WILD CHILD TO COUTURE STYLE

THE Shailah EDMONDS STORY

LYONS PUBLISHING, LTD.
2018

A Memoir

WRITTEN BY: SHAILAH EDMONDS
WITH CHESTER FULTZ

WILD CHILD TO COUTURE STYLE
– The Shailah Edmonds Story

Published by Lyons Publishing, Ltd.
Shailahedmonds.com

ISBN: Paperback: 978-0-9712338-4-3 | Hardbound: 978-0-9712338-3-6

LCCN: 2018902881

Category: Memoir / Autobiography / Fashion Designers / Non-Fiction / African American Models / Models / Modeling / Motivation and Inspiration.

Author: Shailah Edmonds | shailahedmonds@gmail.com

Associate Editor: Chester J. Fultz

Cover Design by: Scott Fowler | Front Cover photo: David Zahner

Makeup: Donyale McCrae

Digital Formatting / Layout by: Eli Blyden | CrunchTime Graphics

Printed in the United States of America

Dedication

This book is dedicated to all of the agents, photographers, fashion designers, (especially in Europe), who saw that special "something" in me and took a chance to help me acquire success in the modeling industry. When I could not earn a living in America as a model because of political limitations, I was welcomed in Europe, being judged only by my genuine authenticity of being my God given beautiful self.

I would have never seen the world or worn so many extravagant ensembles without you.

Contents

Wild Child to Couture Style

Acknowledgments

First and foremost I'd like to thank God for his gift to me, and allowing me to fulfill his plan. There is no thank you big enough for my children, Anthony and KaRon Edmonds, who endured my absence and tumultuous times, and still remained sane and successful. To my first husband Leon Edmonds who held the family together while I followed my fashion journey. To Ruth Turner for changing my life, by noticing my gift, as I walked down the street in Washington, D.C., and sending me to New York City to pursue modeling. To my sister Marian Lyons, who was always there with perpetual encouragement and financial support during my difficult times. She also added editing assistance to this book. To my sister Carolyn Brown, for the family history, and funny family stories, and Cousin Opal Jones, who also contributed greatly to my knowledge of family history. Tabbytha Ferguson was amazing with editing and digitalization of my photos, and thanks to Leonard Davis, Jon Haggins, Billie Blair and others who have inspired and supported me along the way. You know who you are.

Last but certainly not least, my co-writer, Chester J. Fultz, who I know was an angel sent from God. I met him at an Ashford and Simpson concert. There were no more vacant seats on the main floor of the venue, and the host offered me a seat in the balcony. I told her I don't dress like this to sit in the balcony. She was stunned, and found me the only single seat left, which was at Chester's table. Turns out he was also filling a last-minute invitation from a friend, Scott Fowler. He consented to my joining him and Scott's table, and was enamored over my beauty, wardrobe and my story, stating that I should bring a book into fruition, offering to assist with the writing. I'd written it years ago, but his new words brought life, humor and the emphasis it needed, to be historic and a great read. Scott Fowler, who was with him, is responsible for the phenomenal graphics and cover design. I can't thank them enough. There are no accidents in life.

It's been a long road to fruition. I had unexpected success in my singing career, and had to again, put the book on the shelf another few years (Chester was done!) because of practice, lessons, and all that a music career entails.

Finally, in control and realizing my incredible accomplishments as a successful model, I decided it's finally time to display my story of success, sacrifices and hard work, in hopes of encouraging others, and to let the world know that when God has something planned for you, NOTHING can take it away.

Prologue

I'm writing this book so that you may know what it's like for a middle class Black girl from Portland, Oregon, to find herself at the age of 29, (passing for 19), walking the runways of Paris, London, Rome, Milan, Germany, Spain, Portugal, Japan, Finland and Africa, for legendary designers. Yes, I walked and fitted for the real people who created the clothes that woman all over the world clamored to own – Guy Laroche, Dior, Hubert de Givenchy, Valentino, Karl Lagerfeld, and my personal favorite, Yves St. Laurent, just to name the most popular..

I want to give you some idea of what it's like, not only to dwell in that rarefied world, but also to know the hard work, struggles and sacrifices that I endured to get me there, the effect that training and exposure had on me, and how I, as a black woman, influenced the designs and creativity of the most important people in the world of high fashion.

It's quite a task becoming not just a model, but also a very specific, rare breed of model - the type that walks the worlds' most coveted and prestigious runways in the fashion capitals of the world. We like to think of ourselves as thoroughbreds, trained and created for one purpose—to be living mannequins, human displays for the most exquisitely made clothes on earth. We are the bridge, the person who stands as the essential link between the brilliance, skill, talent and sheer genius of great fashion designers, (who possess a vision of what they want a woman to look like when they present their collections to the world), and the women who actually buy the garments, hoping to embody the spirit, if not the style, of the designers themselves. When we "sell" the clothes on the runway, the audience is offered to see what the designer has wrought, and what it would be like to own those beautiful creations for themselves, and, in their imaginations at least, what they would look like in the clothes.

You've seen me before. I know you have. Because if you've ever thumbed through an issue of French or American Vogue, Harpers Bazaar, Ebony, the New York City Newspapers, not to mention the numerous covers of Women's Wear Daily in the early 80's to 90's, you've seen my pictures many times. I'm the tall, elegant girl wearing the couture gown, or the high-energy model with a swirl of fabric around me as I walked. One of the first group of black girls hired by the fashion establishment in Europe when Black models were "in", to work the runways at a time when very few designers—St. Laurent was one of the first—had the vision, the audacity and the courage to want black women in their fashion shows.

I'm going to recount for you what it's like to walk into an atelier for the first time and try to interest a designer in using you to show off his collection, and what it's like to overcome the built-in inhibitions, prejudices, that one has to deal with. How, just by bringing in your perspective and energy to the endeavor, that one is able to influence the vision and, yes, the creativity, of these masters of fabric and design. How I was able to introduce the beauty of kinky hair, something as foreign as an abstract shaped Afro, to the mainstream world of beauty, fashion and advertising. How, with all the odds and obstacles against me, with the perseverance and drive of a raging ram, I managed to achieve the dreams of my desire. But I'm getting ahead of myself.

Let me back up and start at the beginning of my career, back before I knew what a "Dior turn" meant, back before I learned how to "sell" the clothes, back before I even knew what an atelier was, let alone where to find one. Before the model's stance and bearing her carriage and walk, became an inextricable part of my life, and back before I met the person who would introduce me to a world that I scarcely knew existed, but that would change my life forever.

Wild Child to Couture Style

CHAPTER ONE

The Humble Beginning

There are many times, even today when a total stranger will stop me on the street, a social setting, in a department store, or wherever, and remark on my carriage. Invariably, they want to know if I studied ballet, or was a dancer at some point. I just smile and reply, "no, I never studied ballet, but I modeled for many years". The person will usually say something like, "I thought so—there's something about you". I'm always grateful for the compliment, and that so many years of rigorous training have never left me, but I also have to laugh when I recount for myself how difficult it was for me to learn the "model" walk and stance, and how uncoordinated I was in the beginning.

If anyone has told you to "stand up straight, stop slouching, tuck in your butt", or words to that effect, listen, because I had to hear those words thousands of times before I was ready to strut my stuff on the catwalk. And let me assure you, as someone who would wind up walking the most prestigious runways in the world, I was a gangly teen with rounded shoulders and bad posture. I thank my mother who constantly whacked me in the back, while telling me to stand up straight. This was only one aspect of my inauspicious, (and unlikely) beginning.

I suppose many of us have to contend with what are euphemistically referred to as "dysfunctional families". I know I did. I was born in Portland, Oregon, the third of four children. During the course of my childhood, I had to contend with alcoholic parents, a battered mother, and a father who, though there was no such diagnosis at the time, was also clearly a sex addict. We lived in a predominantly black neighborhood, in rural Portland, Oregon, in a lovely two-story, three-bedroom house, complete with a garage, a backyard, and a dog. We also had a basement where my father built swings for us, and I'd spend many times alone there, watching the spiders and dreaming. It was also there I'd create my first movie on a Give-A-Show projector toy, after which I charged my friends ten cents to watch, while I narrated. Oh how I loved that cool, peaceful, solitary basement, where my imagination could run wild!

My mother, born Myrtle Jones, from Shreveport, Louisiana, was a stay at home mom, diligently taking care of the cooking, cleaning and household duties, until we were much older. Her Great-Great Grandmother Mamie Cecile Prudhomme, was the wife of Gregoire Francois, who both lived in Natchitoches, Louisiana. Her Grandmother Clarise Jones, a mother of twelve children, with Grandfather Dave Jones (who had three wives and eight other children), was the matriarch of the entire Jones clan, and deemed a very wise and distinguished woman. Dave was a successful businessman who owned a grocery store and ferry service. My mother was raised by her aunt, after her mother Victoria Bivens, from Marshall, Texas, and her father, Elmo Jones from Shreveport, La, both died mysteriously, and young. She was a striking 5'10" buxom beauty that doted on my domineering fathers every word and need, though there were constant arguments between them. Most often her conversations to the children would begin with "Yo daddy says..." which from a very young age, annoyed me. I always wished she were stronger and more independent.

My father, Dock Lyons Jr., a heavily built 6'2" handsome man, also from Shreveport, was very mechanically inclined and migrated to Portland in the early 1940's, to work in the shipyards and the railroads. By the time I was born, he worked a night shift at a bank as head of the custodial department, while sometimes maintaining a second job during the day. He never spoke of his family history. Through pictures and relatives, I realized his Great Grandmother Tillie, was born into slavery, and not much was known about his Grandmother Beaulah Johnson, who was a very stylish woman, or his dapper Grandfather Mr. Johnson. Tecora Johnson, his mother, who was named after a slave ship, (The Tecora), inherited her mothers' style, and was a schoolteacher, as well as an avid violinist. Her husband, Dock Lyons Sr, was also a very stylish, handsome man and mechanically inclined. My father was a hardworking proud person, never admitting to us that he was a janitor, or his father, a chauffeur. He kept the family well dressed and fed, and had a wicked sense of humor. His favorite outing for us on Sundays was to take us for a ride in the country or to the airport to watch the planes take off and land, which I also found fascinating, and somewhat magical. On rare occasions, we went to drive-in movies in the remote countryside, where I would stare at the stars, always looking for the Big and Small Dipper constellations, and more than once, saw strange lights in a V or circular formation, appear and disappear suddenly. I always kept those sightings to myself as my secret connection to the universe. I remember standing on my father's feet as he danced me around the room, and pony rides on his back, until he collapsed. I was told that I was born left handed, and he bound my left hand behind me as a toddler, forcing me to be right handed. His reasoning was, that I was going to have enough problems being black, let alone left handed, which I never understood until much later. Family members mentioned he played piano, though he never admitted to being a pianist or wanting to talk about his musical endeavors. I later learned he had short little fingers on both hands that couldn't reach the keys, which stifled any career possibilities. He still remained an avid jazz enthusiast, and we grew up listening to all of his collected albums by the greats, which I still own today. We would watch foreign films together which gave me my first ear for the German and French language. His main focus, however, was on his car, which he bought brand new, with cash, every two years, drove like a maniac, and cherished more than anything. For family vacation a few times, we'd drive from Portland through the hot desert (with no air conditioning in the car) to Shreveport, Louisiana to visit his mother, whom we called Mamoo. Our family joke was when I (who was so skinny) was sleeping on the floor of the car, got stuck under the front seat. It took my family hours, on the desert to get me out! Though he had a fun and generous side to him, he was just as abusive and mean on the other side, and everyone in the family feared him.

My parents were drinkers and smokers, and I was 12 or 13 when I stole my first beer from them and drank the entire can. I got so sick and began vomiting non-stop. Around that time I'd also sneak cigarettes and smoke in the basement, which made me feel so grown. (Parents, note your children are always watching you!) Of course I got the punishment of my life for both incidents. Maybe it was my thinking, but it seems, as an adolescent, I got more whippings and punishments than any of my siblings. Oh the memories in that house.

Unlike the rest of my siblings, who had full bodies, flat features and bigger frames, I was very long and thin. From a Southern standpoint, my parents thought I was emaciated and were always trying to force feed me, or give me special drinks to fatten me up, to no avail. Although all of us were born two years apart, we didn't grow up as a close-knit family. Probably from all the chaos of our parents, and being ignored by them, we kind of stayed to ourselves, bickered with each other, and had more fun with our friends, than with each other.

I never had a birthday party, or extracurricular activities as a young a child, so I buried myself in books to not get bored. Around the age of six or seven, I also found joy in watching the old black and white movies with all the glamorous movie stars, and their exquisite fashion, after which I would walk around the house in my mother's high heels, playing movie star. I would also put on four or five pair of socks and a big comforter on the floor and play ballerina, displaying my love of the arts, to no avail. Whenever I was asked what I wanted to be when I grew up, with my two front teeth missing, I would reply "A movin' sthar!" (My family reminded me of that during the height of my modeling career). I would often write poems for my father, and hide them under his pillow, another sure sign I had a God-given talent for the arts, but alas, ignored again. Often times, usually during our family dinner, which we always had together, I would daydream intensely, or go into these "trances" as my parents called them, staring off into space for five to ten minutes, imagining myself as a big star in movies with beautiful clothes, or a prima ballerina. My parents always brought me back to reality, with a thump on the back of my head. Little did I realize then, that I was harnessing my metaphysical gift to my fate, and a strong spiritual connection to my world of future blessings. Envision your dreams!

Through it all, despite being battered, whipped and confused, my mother managed to take my two older sisters, Carolyn and Marian, one younger brother Douglas and me to Sunday school and church religiously every Sunday, and the Lyons family upheld a respectable reputation. Anybody who knows anything about the black church understands that means I was in church from 9 in the morning until 2 in the afternoon. After Sunday school, I either sat through a sermon, most of which I didn't understand a word of or rarely listened to, and slow boring hymns that I always wished they would speed up. Once a month I sang in the junior choir during the main sermon, where I longed to be chosen as a soloist, but was always kept in the back of the group, because I was so tall. It was here my sister Carolyn recognized my natural fashion sense. One Sunday there was no heat in the church, and the choir members were instructed to keep their coats on under their robes. The robes had a close fitting white collar around the neck, and everyone put the robe completely over their coats. My coat had a full fur shawl collar, which was too big to fit under the robe, so I pulled it out over the top of the robe. I was the only one with a fur trimmed choir robe!

Twice I got punished, and sometimes whippings for sneaking around the corner to the Pentecostal church between services, where the music was jumping, people were dancing in the aisles, and the tambourines were shaking, I just loved that music, but after the whippings I decided to stop attending. I was truly the rebel in the family.

By 9 years old, I so badly wanted to play the piano; its music just moved me to the bones. I'd asked my parents for lessons, but I was the third child and they'd spent money on lessons for my older sisters who didn't take it seriously, so when it was my turn, they simply said, "No more money wasted on music lessons!" They hadn't a clue that I possessed a great ear for music, nor how I truly loved that instrument. (Parents can sometimes be the best dream killers.) So the headstrong Aries that I was, began sneaking piano lessons from my best friend Rosie Taylor, who lived nearby. She dreaded her lessons, and was glad to teach me what she knew. One Sunday during early service, the church pianist was ill, and they asked if anyone in the audience could play the song, "Jesus Keep Me Near The Cross", the very song I'd been practicing with Rosie! My hand shot up and my mother gasped with shock, but before she could say anything or grab me, I was hightailing it up to the altar where the piano was. I made it through the verses playing lightly, but was especially loud during the chorus, which I knew well. Was that not enough to show my parents that I had a love for the arts and show business, and not shy about it? Apparently not, it was talked about around the house for a few days and slowly forgotten, then back to the same routine.

Being in church the entire day felt like torture then. Even so, old habits, good ones and bad, die hard. To this day I keep a bible by my bedside, a piano at home, and pray all the time (even throughout my worldly travels). I'm convinced my connection to my spirituality is what has kept me alive, sane and successful all these years.

CHAPTER TWO

The Tween Years

I was around 11, when one day my father came home with new bicycles for all the children. Mine was a red Schwinn, my favorite color, and oh how I loved that bicycle. Rosie and I would travel all over Portland, from one end of the river to the other on our bikes. There was nothing at the time that was more freeing, and beautiful, than to feel that breeze against my face and fiercely riding into unknown territory. I would find refuge, and escape from any worries or boredom, on my bike...until a few times, I took it too far. I hated ironing, and one beautiful, perfect-for-bike-riding day, my mother gave me a huge basket of clothes to iron. I pouted and moaned, as I slithered out the back door, grabbed my bike, riding out into the wild, not returning for hours. In the last year of elementary school we were required to learn to cook and sew, and how I loved my patient and kind home economics teacher, Mrs. Shrock. I loved sewing especially, EXCEPT for zippers. They were hell, and it always took me two or three efforts to get it right. One day while putting the finishing touches on a beautiful pleated skirt, the zipper just wasn't happening, so I threw the skirt under my bed, grabbed my bike and went riding off again, to who knows where. Well, needless to say, I got whipped and punished on both occasions when I returned; lesson learned, you may be able to run away from your problems temporarily, but eventually you have to face them. Nevertheless, I still enjoyed many more good years on what I called my "red jet".

At 14, the State of Oregon bought our property to build a highway, so we had to relocate. My father had a great business mind, and was able to pay cash, $14,000, for our new ranch style, 3-bedroom home, on the corner, in a totally white neighborhood. I had just graduated elementary school where I was President of the student body, and quite respected. Now, to be separated from all my friends, and begin high school, in a new neighborhood, was quite overwhelming, yet exciting. I entered Jefferson High School in awe of so many white people in one place, and where I was a face among what seemed like thousands. I gradually became comfortable when I found some of my old friends, but I noticed immediately that the white people were nice, but didn't mix with us often or for any long period. They actually slightly feared the black students, never talking back to us, and steered clear of any confrontation with immediate apologies. (That was the first rude awakening when I later came to the East coast; white people actually talked back to you, and didn't back away so easily!) I slowly acclimated to my new high school world rather well.

The first summer after my freshman year, I was asked to babysit for my cousin Marie, who was recently divorced and lived in a large 2 story house in the black neighborhood, with her four children, 3 boys and a girl. I enjoyed the well-behaved children, who on my first day told me their house was haunted. Around lunchtime every day, we would sit very still and listen to the stairs creak one at a time, as the ghost went up the stairs. There were always strange noises upstairs, which everybody ignored, and Marie gave me sound advice NOT to go into the room where the ghosts were. That room was forbidden to everybody. Well, you know I'm a hardheaded Aries, and one day, I put the kids down for a nap and quoted, like the movie says, "I ain't afraid of no ghosts!" and headed up to the room. I entered slowly, quietly closing the door behind me, and just stood in front of the twin beds, that were never used. I remind you, it was summer, but it was about thirty degrees in that room…so cold. I just stood there, and suddenly a book falls off the shelf. Though the window wasn't opened, I assured myself it was just the wind, while standing my ground. Then the curtain started moving, and I heard scuffling noises behind the closet door. Well so much for not being afraid, I hightailed it out of there so fast, never to return, and every so often listened, with bugged eyes as the ghosts took their daily walk on the stairs.

The star football player of my high school, Joe Jackson lived in the neighborhood where I babysat. He would often speak to me, and every time he saw me, he became friendlier. I was in heaven! Joe Jackson, talking to me? He was every high school girls dream guy, and I admit I got a little fuzzy when we talked. One afternoon, to my ultimate surprise, he appeared at the door of Marie's house. I cracked open the door to talk to him, and he barged in, shouting at all the kids to get out and go play outside. They were terrified, as I shouted, "What are you doing?" He slammed the door after them, grabbed me and threw me to the floor, covering my mouth and ripping off my pants. As he raped me, I began to cry, saying that I was a virgin. He became terrified and asked why I didn't tell him. What a stupid question after he'd assaulted me! We got up off the floor to see a big stain of blood on the carpet, and I began to wail. I told him if he helped me clean it up, I wouldn't tell on him. Well we scrubbed and vacuumed like maniacs until the stains were gone, but then, the phone rang. It was Marie, who said a neighbor had called her at work, to say her children were running wild in the street. I told her I'd call her right back and darted out to get the kids. When we returned, Joe sheepishly left, and I called Marie back, saying I got carried away cleaning, and all was well. She replied, "Well who was that man seen coming out of the house?" I was busted big time. Gawd, did I dread going home that day, but my mother, though hurt and disappointed, was so cool when I told her the story. Thank God, she didn't tell my father, and I was allowed to finish my babysitting job.

I was a good student throughout my early years in school and showed great leadership qualities until I was about 16. Outsiders told me several times that I was a pretty girl, but I never thought so. I was a tall, lanky teen with beautiful hair, and was totally insecure, because I hadn't developed big breasts or a butt as my girlfriends had, and never got attention from the boys. (My measurements at 13 years old were 19-19-19). Olive Oyl was my constant nickname. Ultimately, as a sophomore, I was pretty much forcing myself upon boys at school, one in particular, a fast talking slickster named Jackie Scott. This action was totally from peer pressure, because all of my girlfriends had so-called boyfriends, especially, my now well-developed best friend Rosie, who had them waiting in line. Jackie began giving me attention, though I always thought it was out of pity. One day Jackie's crew of guy friends decided to skip school with my crew of girlfriends. We decided to meet at his aunt's house, while she was away at work. The guys managed to smuggle in lots of booze and having never drank before, I indulged, got totally and completely wasted, and of course had sex. What an extravaganza! I passed out and was awakened by my friends at 3PM, the time school was over. Boy, did they have a hard time sobering me up! After a cold shower and gallons of water, I made it home at my usual time, explaining to my parents I wasn't feeling well, and went straight to bed.

I wasn't allowed to date yet, because the rule in our house was no dating until you were 18 years old. But I was in love (I thought), ready to bust out of the gate, and no one was going to stop me. Jackie and I secretly met a few times after school, slowly developing a comfortable relationship. My girlfriend and classmate Kassandra lived in the neighborhood, and my mother would let me visit her on weekends. Little did she know on my visits to Kassandra's house, Jackie would pick me up on the corner in his souped up '57 Chevy, and we'd ride around snuggling, and always ended up in the same secluded spot making wild love in the back seat. But when summer came, our trysts came to a screeching halt, because he had to begin working for his uncle, and I had an offer to go to a college prep summer program at the University of Oregon, in Eugene, Oregon, for six weeks.

CHAPTER THREE

The Bump

Being away, I now realized Jackie and I weren't in love at all, it was just something to do, due to peer pressure, so I began losing myself in my books. We were paired with study partners at the University, and I was paired with a very handsome, intelligent guy, named Ben Fluker, (pronounced Flooker) with whom I got along with fabulously. We soon began dating, and he began to fall in love. I wish he hadn't, because by then I realized I hadn't seen my period in nearly two months. It was there and then that I realized, I was pregnant with Jackie's child. When I called Jackie to break the news to him, he simply replied we'd just have to deal with it when I returned to Portland. Nice. Now, how was I to deal with the bigger obstacles ahead?

Obstacle one: How to break it to Ben gently? I finally mustered up the courage one night after a few beers. Nice guy that he was, he took it with ease, still wanting to stick with me, knowing my feelings for Jackie had waned. That was true love!

Obstacle two: How to hide it from my parents? I had to figure out what the hell to do.

Those six weeks in summer school seemed to fly by, and by now I'd developed a little bump of a stomach. My parents picked me up from campus and the first thing my mother says is "Oh, you finally gained some weight there! I never thought I'd see the day!" I just smiled. I was back at home a few weeks, and things were going smoothly, secret still intact, with no plans of what to do about my situation, when again, fate stepped in.

It was an early summer evening, and I was preparing to meet my friends for a party. I had just finished my shower, doing my hair and make-up, wearing a light robe, and slippers. As I passed my mother, the wind blew my robe open, exposing my stomach. "Girl, you pregnant?" my mother screamed. I sheepishly replied yes, and she asked, "How far? "About six months" I quietly replied. "SIX MONTHS! OH MY GOD!" she yelled, "Just wait until your daddy gets home...he's going to kill you!" Oh hell no, I thought, and without missing a beat, ran out of the house, clad in my robe and slippers, and I never stopped running. I just ran, not knowing where I was going. I finally stopped at a phone booth, borrowed a coin from a stranger, and called Jackie who said to come to his house. Upon arrival, he and his mother greeted me. She sat us down in the living room while asking us what we were thinking about, getting ourselves into this mess, and what we wanted to do. We just looked at each other in silence, like the two dumb lost lambs that we were. She finally asked him if he wanted to marry me, and he said no!!!!! My mouth fell open in shock as I realized he didn't love me either, and I hastily asked to use the phone. I called my girlfriend Delores (Dee) Drokes, whose parents were older, and went to bed early. I told her the situation, and she said to come right over, her parents were asleep, and she'd sneak me into her bedroom. Jackie drove me there in silence, and sped off as soon as I got out of the car. I began throwing stones at Dee's window, and she immediately peeked out and gave me the signal she was coming to open the door. When the door opened, it was not Dee standing there, but her parents. I nearly peed on myself. To this day, it's still hard for me to forgive her for that. I was devastated, but it was probably for the best, because her parents were good listeners. They listened to my story, gave me good advice, and let me stay the night. Of course I rolled my eyes at Dee and didn't speak to her all night.

The next morning, heeding the advice of Dee's parents, I called home. My mother sounded horrible, and said to come home. I made her promise that she or my dad would not beat me. I arrived home and went straight to my bedroom in total fear of anticipating what was to come next. My mother came into my room and said that my dad refused to let me stay in the house while pregnant with an illegitimate child, and they had made arrangements for me to live with my cousin Marie, for whom I used to babysit.

Marie was my first cousin by marriage, who had by this time, moved from the haunted house and remarried an ex-serviceman, Mac. She was a beautiful mulatto woman with freckles and a kind heart and voice. We got along fabulously, me sharing the household duties and again, babysitting her four children. My mother visited frequently, suggesting at one point that I give the baby up for adoption, being that I was so young and had my whole life ahead of me. Being the dominating Aries that I am, I flatly refused, because I knew I was grown, (as every 17 year old does), and could handle it. How could I feel something growing inside of me, and just give it away? No way! You could see in her face that she was concerned, and saddened by the fact that I would not agree, and could not live at home during this traumatic time. During her last visit she predicted that I'd deliver on the next full moon. She was right. On November 15th, I was in the hospital with Jackie and my mother by my side, where I delivered Anthony, a bouncing baby boy.

After living with Marie for another 3 months, my father decided to forgive me, and invited me to come back home. A very hard decision for me to make, but I decided to accept, especially because I was beginning to feel very uncomfortable with Marie's husband Mac, who was becoming just a bit too friendly. So, there I was, back at my parent's house, barely speaking to my father, who eventually became so fond of Anthony, I could rarely separate them. What a hypocrite! My parents slowly began to help care for Anthony, which allowed me a little freedom, so I went to night school, and was able to go back to high school and graduate with my class. Ben Fluker even escorted me to my senior prom!

So high school was over, what was I to do now? There was so much drinking and fighting between my parents at this point, they didn't care, and there was not even a whisper from them about college. So I got a job at the telephone company, where my older sister Carolyn had left a great impression as a former employee. After a few months of work, I decided to get an apartment with my girlfriend Kassandra. When I told my mother, she enthusiastically said, "Great, and to please hurry, because your father is starting to get an erection every time you come around". The hate and fear that welled up inside of me, after hearing those words, was irrepressible, and at that point I realized he had a bigger problem than I ever realized.

CHAPTER FOUR

On My Own

Kassandra had a beautiful body, a tough girl demeanor, with a sweet raspy voice, who could convince anyone to side with her on just about anything. She would always hustle to keep a job and was very street smart. Though I felt safe with her, I didn't like her boyfriend or the crowd he hung with. We found a cute two-bedroom apartment, and moved in with my son Anthony in tow. Oh, did we have fun decorating, cooking together, and she was a big help in teaching Anthony how to walk, again with that convincing voice and manner. For about six months, things couldn't have been better; I'd even bought myself a car, an old Pontiac with a big Indian chief head on the hood. Seems as soon as I got the car, the boys started hanging around, firstly Kassandra's boyfriend, who brought with him a few pimps, and their women. On one occasion, he brought a guy to meet me, named Ronald "Iceman" Collier, a very handsome smooth talking guy, who easily became my boyfriend. Well, the parties started with the entire group of street people, and would sometimes go on for days at a time. I think Kassandra and I were the only ones with a real job, and sure enough within a few months, because of the late parties nearly every night, we were either late or missed work totally. We eventually lost our jobs, couldn't pay the rent, and none of the so-called boyfriends or friends offered to help. Ronald had wrecked my car, and left it on the side of the road somewhere, and the apartment was a disaster. We started hanging out until the wee hours of the morning with these bandits, and one night even ended up in jail after one of the girls got in trouble with the police. After this, I exploded, and had it out with Kassandra, telling her we had to get rid of everybody, and get ourselves back together. She agreed and within a week, we had broken our ties with those hoodlums. We had our peace back, but we were so far behind in bills, and unemployed, it seems we would never catch up, but we were determined to figure a way out. After some frivolous suggestions, I suggested we get another roommate until we get back on our feet. My friend Carolyn Gibson was looking to get out of her parents' house, and Kassandra agreed that she'd be a good choice, because of her levelheaded demeanor. Carolyn accepted our offer, not knowing of course how much trouble we were in, and agreed to pay a month's security, and a month's rent up front. Perfect! Just what we needed to catch up on everything! Carolyn moved in, and Kassandra and I nervously helped her unpack while making small talk, and trying to have fun. Just as we finished unpacking the last box...the lights went out. Busted!!! We hadn't paid the electricity bill in months. We had to confess just how much trouble we were in, and Carolyn was livid and wanted no part of it, or us. She packed up, demanded her money back, and moved out the next day. Kassandra and I had to move back home as well, a place where I totally did not want to be.

* * *

Now, with a child in tow, my dreams of being an actress, ballerina or singer were totally ignored, and out of the question. Do I dare even mention to my parents that my artistic desires were overflowing? No way!! My parents insisted nursing or teaching would be a more sensible career, especially at this point. So with my son and I living back at home, I began to ponder these suggestions, and decided; first and foremost, to begin, I needed a college education and a degree to accomplish any type of career. I contacted my high school counselor who told me about a scholarship program at the University of Portland, where I could live on campus. I jumped at the opportunity, and my mother helped make babysitting plans for Anthony.

Not long after I was home, my old beau Ronald, the "Iceman" made an attempt to visit me at my parent's home. I opened the door to greet him, and in a matter of minutes, my father arrived at the door, gun in tow, giving Ronald five seconds to get off his property, and never come back. Of course Ronald fled, and that's the last I ever heard or saw of him. Dear God, was I glad to get out of that house!

I barely made it through a year and a half of college at the University of Portland, as an elementary education major. I studied hard, but partied just as hard, and my grades favored the latter. During that time, my girlfriend Rosie introduced me to Leon Edmonds, a star basketball player for Portland State College. Very nice guy, but a little slow, compared to the street-smart fast talkers I was used to, however, negotiations were in the works for him to be drafted into the professional ABA basketball league, for the Virginia Squires. We dated for about a year, my parents liked him, he got along with Anthony, and to my great surprise and relief, he proposed! He wanted to take me and my son, to live with him in his home town, Washington, D.C. Without missing a beat, I accepted, and all I could think about was "Thank you, Jesus, I'm leaving Portland!" By this time my mother had given me my first marijuana joint. An orderly at the hospital where she was currently working told her if I wanted to be in the arts, I should try it. Wow, what a feeling! I was in heaven and felt I could conquer the world, so I was more than ready for a change. I couldn't wait. New beginnings and travel to this day give me such energy, and are always so exciting. In a matter of months, I had my life packed in a few suitcases, and was bursting with anxiety to leave. Just before leaving, I heard that Ben Fluker had been killed trying to rob a gas station, dressed in women's clothing! The newspaper said that he did it to dodge the military draft. That was so unlike him, and so very sad.

CHAPTER FIVE

Getting Out of Dodge

It was early July and I was in a complete state of ecstasy, and acute anticipation during my trip to Washington DC. Upon arrival, I exited the airport to be engulfed by a heat that I'd never felt before, I felt as if I was suffocating. "What's wrong with the air?" I asked Leon, "I feel like I'm in a steam room!"

"It's called humidity." He snidely answered. From day one I hated it, and still do today.

We lived with Leon's mother for about a month during which time we found a Justice of the Peace and had a private ceremony of marriage. Leon began showing early signs of jealousy. He went through my belongings and found my diary with stories of my early boyfriend attractions from age 14, and took it out to a huge field and threw it as far as he could into the tall grass. I was very hurt, being the writer I am, and thinking of all those lost memories, but got over it eventually, focusing on my new life. We finally moved into a very small apartment across the street from Leon's mother. I hated it, not only because it was too close for any long term privacy, but also because it was a walkup with small green drab rooms that looked like jail cells. Also, each time I sat down at the kitchen table to eat, a spider would lower itself from the light fixture above. Leon realized it was also too small for the three of us, and thankfully, two months later we moved two blocks away, to a nicer apartment, which was a bit more spacious.

I suppose many young people with stars in their eyes, and their heads in the clouds don't really understand what marriage really entails. Statistically, we were no different—as a very young married couple we respected one another, worked hard and managed to keep it together for three years. After a year or so, however, I realized Leon was a hoarder, constantly piling up memorabilia from all of his life into one closet, in total disorder. It depressed me each time I saw the mountain of "stuff". By this time his contract for professional basketball was cancelled due to his knee problems, and he refused to have the required surgery. We were also growing apart; he liked to go fishing and the simple things a quiet life would entail, and I liked the nightlife, fun parties, being social, networking. He began to heavily follow the Muslim religious beliefs, and wanted me to join him, but I would have no part of it. Somehow we tolerated each other, and on one occasion he took me on a day trip to shop at Macy's in New York City. New York City! I was beside myself, a place I'd only seen in the movies, I was now going to visit? I couldn't wait. Upon arrival, I was overwhelmed with amazement at the tall buildings, the people, the hustle and bustle; totally opposite of life in Portland or D.C. I walked through Macys, with bulging eyes, overwhelmed at all of the incredibly great fashion. I bought a pair of red suede clogs, which I cherished for years. Leon recognized my immense adoration of the city, and immediately whisked me back to the car, and before I knew it, was on the road back to D.C.

So life went on as usual, we eventually had a son KaRon, (named after the Muslim holy book, though spelled differently) and were living a typical suburban life, until I just couldn't take it anymore. I realized we needed to go our separate ways. Nice guy that he was, Leon had even legally adopted Anthony, so we'd all have the same last name, but he was also becoming even more jealous and controlling. We both had good jobs, me, again, at the telephone company, as a customer service representative, and he with the city recreation department. We had a healthy family lifestyle, but I was totally bored, and he knew it. He began to sense me distancing myself from him, and began to get abusive and violent. I was becoming afraid and miserable, and had to figure out a way to get out of this relationship.

* * *

I was working at C&P Telephone Company in downtown Washington, D.C., a nice, good paying job with great co-workers, whom I enjoyed. One day, it was business as usual, until my supervisor brought in a new employee to tour our office, before starting his position. I was sure he was specifically carved from stone by Jesus Christ himself, and sent from God especially for me, because my mouth literally dropped open, and I got chills just looking at him. This man was FINE!!! I stared at him for a while and got a receptive glance from him as well. His name was Charles Patrick Wood, 6'5", and a former army reserve serviceman with a great build.

That following week, we met in the company lounge, on one of our breaks. I found him intelligent, sensible, witty, quickly responding to my conversation with all the right words at the right time, and just plain gorgeous. Needless to say, we definitely were attracted to one another, and after a few months of settling into his job, we would meet daily after work for drinks. He was living with his girlfriend in his mother's house with their two children, and was just as bored as I was. We began pouring our stories out to each other, and he became genuinely interested in my situation and me. We could never show any public affection, due to our co-workers and our situations, so one day after work we decided to get a room to have a short tryst. I thought Charles was so worldly because he knew so many things about Washington DC (worldly ☺) and could organize things in a heartbeat. He knew of a boarding house that would ask us no questions upon check-in, and we planned a day to meet there after work. We arrived simultaneously to a huge white house, and after registering, were escorted to a large but quaint, cozy room, complete with a fireplace! Immediately after closing the door to the room, we embraced and began snuggling. OMG what a great kisser and package that man had! I was thrilled!!! After we lit the fireplace, things got heated up really quickly, and it had nothing to do with the fireplace! But each time we were about to get into the act, his erection died! I asked him what in the world the matter could be, and as his eyes welled up with tears, he replied he'd never been so excited, or felt so right with anyone, and he thought he loved me. So he just wanted to hold me and savor the moment, which we did for the entire hour as we watched the cackling fire.

Meanwhile, things were getting worse with Leon and me, especially now that I'd been, too often, late picking up the children from the sitter after work, and had alcohol on my breath nearly every day, (Charles was a big drinker). I realized now that I had to get away from Leon sooner than later, so instead of meeting Charles after work, my after work duty now changed to researching apartments. It didn't take me long to find a nice garden apartment in Suitland, Maryland, which Charles agreed to help me move in to.

The abuse from Leon was getting even worse, and Charles became very concerned with what I was going through, especially when I showed up to work one day with a bruise on my face. Charles believed a man should NEVER hit a woman, and he was furious. He was also concerned about my fear of how I would leave without getting hurt, so together, we made plans for the great escape from Leon.

We both called in sick from work on the chosen moving day, and Charles rented a U-Haul truck. We arrived at my apartment early and worked like crazed maniacs, packing boxes and throwing things in piles and putting it wherever we could. In a matter of hours, it was done, and we drove away like Bonnie and Clyde. Upon arrival to the new apartment, Charles along with my friend Rosemary, who lived nearby, just as hastily, unpacked the truck, and left me to organize things.

Rosemary's boyfriend Larry, was Leon's friend as well, and Rosemary told me Leon had come home from work only to find maybe a few pieces of silverware, and that he was very furious and hurt when he called. Overall the transition went rather smoothly. No one would tell him where I'd moved, but Leon, finally, within a week, found me. After a few futile attempts to reconcile, (once nearly raping me), he finally realized I didn't love him anymore, and left me in peace. Except for one time, my friend Sandy, who didn't know about Charles, had set me up on a blind date, which I reluctantly accepted. As he was bringing me home that evening, a car swerved in front of us, blocking the car. It was Leon, who jumped out of the car, pulled my date out and began beating him bloody. As Leon left, I was a screaming maniac, frantically apologizing to my date, which of course, I never heard from again. I also realized it was a set-up, because Sandy's ex-boyfriend was Leon's best friend. I was so glad it wasn't Charles that Leon beat up! I truly loved this guy.

My friend Rosemary was what we called a professional booster. She could steal anything, and get away with it. She was such a sweet sensible girl, had a nice job, but just had this habit that made me quite nervous. She would bring me new things every day that she had stolen, to furnish my new apartment, including food! Filet mignon, pork chops, even a ham! Though I appreciated the help, I finally had to ask her to stop bringing me things.

I found a wonderful babysitter for my youngest son KaRon, named Elaine, who lived just across the street from my apartment, She always had a houseful of happy children, and my son fit in perfectly. I also found a great school that bussed Anthony to and from home, door to door. Things couldn't have worked out more perfectly.

My apartment was very comfortable and peaceful, with a terrace overlooking a cemetery, and Charles would visit frequently. We had become very comfortable together. Somehow his girlfriend found my address, and one day came to look for him during one of his visits. Charles hid in the closet, (classic), while I cursed her out, even taunting her about not being able to keep her man. Charles and I had a big laugh afterwards, because I actually let her into my apartment to show her he wasn't there, and Charles said he nearly peed his pants! Our lovemaking by then had become so amazingly and ridiculously awesome that there was no turning back, and that day he decided to move in with me. Of course there was drama on his side as well, but things went relatively smoothly, and we began a nice life, driving to work together while snuggling, being on the bowling team together, (he was really a pro), and making fun plans.

CHAPTER SIX

The Game Changer

I acquired a love of fashion early, from my mother who loved to shop, and was always dressed impeccably. From pictures I saw of my Grandmother, I realized she too had a keen eye for fashion. She worked for a rich lady who owned a clothing boutique in Shreveport, Louisiana, who also had three female children the exact ages of my sisters and I. She would give my Grandmother clothing her children had outgrown (hand-me-downs), and we would often receive boxes of expensive, stylish clothing from my Grandmother when we were young. I would get overly excited when the box of clothing would arrive from her, and I was always the first to tear it open, grabbing at garments and putting outfits together. From this, I developed my own style, (get it models?), and really enjoyed looking different, and standing out from the crowd.

I went to work dressed a bit differently than the average office worker, or so I was told. In retrospect, I guess I did! How do you like this for an outfit; a strapless party dress with a crinoline, or this one; platform shoes, (they were very big and high in those days), a pink denim pantsuit with a midriff blouse that showed quite a bit of bare tummy! Yes to the office! I was 5'10" tall in my stocking feet, and to top it all off, I sported the biggest Afro the world had ever seen, all of which meant that I must have been 6'4", by the time you accounted for everything. By this time I'd also acquired a love of thrift shopping with my gay co-worker, Dennis, and mixing the old with the new. Let's just say, I was hard to miss. Still, I didn't think I stood out particularly, and felt no different from anyone else, other than I was taller than most, however, I was very secure with my look. Apparently recognizing this security, several of my friends encouraged me to go into modeling. Turns out, they were right about the attire, (little did I know then I had created my own "style"), but totally misread the fact that I was secure about my body. But I thought about it and decided, hey, why not? I was getting bored with my job, and the more I thought about it, the better the prospect seemed.

Then, fate intervened. Though I had no idea at the time, I was about to meet someone who would change my life completely.

I was walking down K Street in Northwest D.C. one day, on my way back to work from lunch, when a strikingly beautiful black woman approached, rushing over to me. She asked me if I knew I was slouching, walking in my platform shoes with my head down. I reluctantly answered negatively. She introduced herself as Ruth Turner, and after inquiring about what plans I had for my life, told me that I needed to stand up straight and be proud of my height at all times. She suggested that I consider modeling and offered to give me modeling instructions. You talk about a Godsend! Ruth Turner turned out to be the person who, more than anyone else is responsible for setting me on the road to becoming a professional model. Ruth formerly owned a modeling school, knew people in the modeling field in New York, and currently managed a boutique next door to my office. She graciously offered to help me get started in the modeling business, but when reality struck, I was just a bit reluctant. The security of my job, my lifestyle with Charles and my children had now become so comfortable, so I told her I would think about it.

Meanwhile, friends at work had recommended me to people like Tee Taylor and Ron Cooke who were doing local, small shows in nightclubs, social events and department store shows. I finally began to get my feet wet with these small shows, and began to dream about making it big, getting into the field for real. That meant one thing—going to New York City and trying my hand at modeling there. I just knew I was, "ready", you know. Boy, did I have a lot to learn!

I thought about Ruth's offer, decided I needed her help and called her. I began training with her, still a little reluctant at first, because of the slight insecurity of knowing if I had any real aptitude for "it", whatever "it" turned out to be. And let's face it; I didn't want to be disappointed if it turned out that I was no good at it.

Slowly, gradually, patiently, Ruth coached me in the basics of modeling—runway technique, posture tips, attitude, walking, posing, etc. During our meetings a few times a week in her apartment, she gave me invaluable tips on how to shape my eyebrows, personal hygiene, endless beauty tips, how to take care of my nails, and skin, arrange a portfolio of pictures, etc. She took me to her boutique where we had the most fun shopping, while she was advising me on what styles and colors worked best for me. Advice I desperately needed at that point, though I thought of myself as the most fabulous dresser around!

Do you believe in signs, portents, and invisible forces guiding you in a particular direction? I sure do. Ruth told be about an upcoming modeling competition to be held in New York City, scheduled for the first week in April, sponsored by the World Modeling Association, of which she was a member. She told me that I was ready for my plunge into the modeling ocean, and insisted that I enter the competition. Being that it was my birthday month, I thought it was time for a change. Well! The strictest regimen I had ever endured in my life began at that moment. After I finished my shift at work, we practiced runway technique every night at her apartment. I was so stiff and uncoordinated when it came to doing the Dior full turns, and removing jackets on cue, I couldn't believe it! Slowly I got the hang of it, and after what seemed like weeks of tortuous work, Ruth finally said I was ready. It was only two days before the competition! My sitter Elaine was wonderful and agreed to keep my children for the week. At our final meeting, before giving me registration and spending money, Ruth said one more thing. "You can't go to New York with that plain name of Barbara (my birth name), I was thinking of something exotic like…Shailah". "Shailah" S-h-a-i-l-a-h, I slowly spelled it out, and repeated it several times…"it's fabulous!" I agreed, and before I knew it, I was prepping for my trip the next day, on the Greyhound bus, with a pseudonym, 10 years chopped off of my birthdate, and off to the Big Apple, totally transformed.

CHAPTER SEVEN

Ready or Not, Here I Come!

B efore I left for New York, I called up an old girlfriend of mine from high school in Portland, Oregon, named Paula Ladsen. When Paula first arrived in my class as a transfer from New York city, I noticed she was very smart, outspoken, quick witted, and didn't take anything from the bullies who always tried to pick on newly enrolled people. I admired her strong qualities, immediately wanting to befriend her, and not long after introducing myself, we became fast friends. Though she wasn't that attractive, she had amazingly huge boobs. We chased the boys together, and by our junior year, were pregnant at the same time. She moved back to New York after high school, (her father was a New Yorker), and said I could look her up if ever I came to the city. She was so surprised and excited to hear that I was coming to New York and offered her apartment to me. Upon arrival to New York, I found my way to her apartment, but when she opened the door, I scarcely recognized her! Wow, what a difference the years had made. Paula had put on a lot of weight, was on welfare, had become an alcoholic, and when she smiled most of her teeth were rotten. She was also living with an alcoholic, former drug abusing ex-con, but I had nowhere else to stay, so for the time being, this was home. The city was so cold and dirty to me, but it was all so new, busy and exciting that I loved it!

The next day, I had to report to the Essex House Hotel on Central Park South, where the competition was being held, for orientation and instructions. When I got there and looked around, I tried to calm my nerves, but there were so many people! Ninety-two girls had entered the competition, including Jeanette Cooke, the sister of Ron Cooke from Washington DC, who was a very dramatic model. Although I'd practiced my walks and turns, all the fancy things that Ruth had so patiently taught me, went right out of my head. I dreaded that I might be a disaster, and I was glad Ruth wasn't there to see me. Surprisingly, I met and befriended other girls, even one from Portland, and I was grateful that several of the people I met were very interesting and helpful. But I still felt like a babe in the woods! Before I knew it, and certainly before I felt ready for it, the competition was about to begin. I knew I couldn't be the only one who was so nervous, anxious and irritable, but it sure felt that way. I felt like I was walking in a daze—the whole episode seemed surreal somehow—and I tried to calm myself by checking the important things; my false eyelashes were securely in place, my outfit was perfect, and that I was in my correct assigned place in line. Somehow, don't ask me how, I found myself on stage, but everything that happened after I got there seemed to go by in a blur of activity. All of the girls were required to walk to the microphone, introduce themselves, and walk back and forth across the stage three times; that was it, or at least all I can remember about it. After all the contestants had walked, we sat in the audience, while the judges deliberated for what seemed like an eternity. Finally, it was time to announce the winners and present the awards. I heard screams when other girl's names were called, and I also heard some sobbing around me as well. My heart sank because I hadn't yet heard my name called. I steeled myself; I was determined to take my loss stoically, and not cry until I got back to Paula's house. Suddenly, as if it came from far, far away, I heard someone say, "Shailah

Edmonds, Haute Couture Model of the Year"! I couldn't believe it. I found my knees wobbling as I tried to look as dignified as I could, (and under the circumstances, that wasn't easy, let me tell you), and made it to the stage. A judge asked me once again to demonstrate my walk, so I did while everyone applauded. Then I was handed a huge trophy! I was so nervous. I didn't even know what the words "haute couture" meant! When I got back to my seat, I asked the girl sitting next to me what it meant, and she said, in a heavy southern accent, she thought it meant high fashion, but she wasn't sure. I didn't care if she wasn't sure, I was so proud of my trophy — after the ceremony I rushed to the nearest telephone and called my sister Marian, who I'd confided in throughout my entire transition. "I won high fashion model of the year!" I screamed into the phone, and she screamed back. The next call I made was to Ruth Turner, to thank her for all she had done. She was her cool collected self, and replied matter-of-factly, "I told you so". It was a moment neither of us will ever forget. Suddenly, a woman appeared by my side, told me her name was Judy Foster-Fell, a modeling agent, and that I should give her a call as soon as possible! Could all of this really be happening to me? It seemed incredible, and I was so proud and happy!

Ready or not, I was launched into my modeling career!

CHAPTER EIGHT

Breaking In

W hen I returned to Maryland and burst into my apartment ready to celebrate with Charles, he very stoically congratulated me. "It doesn't seem like you're very happy babe", I said "We're going to New York!" "No, you're going to New York" he replied coldly. "That's no place for me, besides you'll have your career, and no time for me." I was stunned, and tried everything to convince him to go with me, but he wouldn't give in, and after a few days, realizing this was the end of us, he went back to live with his girlfriend. In hindsight he was so right, but at the time, that bittersweet moment just left me numb.

By this time, my parents were totally fed up with me, and wanted nothing to do with my new endeavor. My father said modeling was a career for prostitutes, and my mother always agreed with everything he said, adding that I'd NEVER make it with two children under my belt. (There went my self-esteem!) They refused to even speak to me on the phone, but my Mom did sneak a phone call to me saying if I was going to be in the fashion business, to always 'give 'em a show!' Those words never left me. Bless those of you who have your parents support, it means a lot to a young dreamer.

Ruth Turner suggested I get more pictures for my portfolio before I make my move to New York, so I set up an appointment with a photographer to do some test shots. A test shot is when a photographer and a model need pictures for their portfolios, and there was usually no fee or a very nominal one.

The photographer gets a chance to test new lighting and photo skills, and the model, new poses and styles, (A great way to build a portfolio). I thought I was being so creative and artistic, when I suggested we take the photos in the cemetery, adjacent to my apartment. The photographer loved the idea, so I dressed in my favorite thrift store suit, platform shoes, and cluster curls of my hair on top of my head. We created some beautiful photos, complete with tombstones in the background, that I was so proud of.

Within two weeks of winning the coveted haute couture trophy, on my birthday, I had quit my job at the telephone company, made arrangements with my ex-husband Leon to take care of the children, packed my things in a U-Haul truck and made plans to drive back to New York City to live with Paula. My babysitter Elaine's friend Joyce, kind of a hippie-free spirited type girl, accompanied me on the trip to New York in the U-Haul truck, and helped find a storage place for my belongings. I had researched storage places before I left, and the most reasonable one I found was in Harlem. As we were unloading my TV, a man on the street warned me not to leave it in that place, or it would be stolen. We immediately repacked everything and found another place further downtown.

After settling in with Paula for a few days, I immediately called Judy Foster-Fell, the agent from the competition who asked me to call her, promising to introduce me to all the people I needed to know in the business. My now boyfriend, Pierre who I'd met through Paula, took me to her office in midtown Manhattan. I knew I looked fabulous—I had a new outfit, complete with a matching fedora straw hat, and as always, my indispensable false eyelashes. I just knew this was going to be the opportunity of a lifetime.

The much-anticipated meeting with Judy became, not the opportunity, but the experience of a lifetime, one of the worse experiences in my life. When I walked into her office, and introduced myself, Judy looked at me coldly, and acted as if she had never laid eyes on me before. Crestfallen, I sat down and offered to show her my portfolio. Maybe, I thought, the pictures might jog her memory. She quickly flipped through the pages, barely looking at my pictures, slammed the book closed, raised her eyes and said in a dismissive tone, "Sorry. We have enough black girls right now. If you were white, it would be different." I was flabbergasted. This horrible comment coming from the same woman who, scarcely ten days ago, had praised me for my beauty and elegance!

Even though I was totally in shock at the blatant racist nature of her remark, I managed to find my voice. "I don't quite understand", I replied, in the calmest tone I could muster. "When I met you at the modeling competition two weeks ago, you even invited me to your home, and seemed so willing to help me." She looked at me as if I had taken a leave of my senses. "I don't remember anything of the kind", she said, and stood up as if signaling that this encounter was at an end. I could only stammer, "But, but…" She escorted me to the door, and put her hand directly in my face and said, "I'm sorry, but I'm very busy". Well, needless to say, I was more familiar with the streets than the world of high fashion, at that point; also I am an Aries. Not only was I not about to leave gracefully, but also was determined to have the last word. Enraged and insulted, I could feel the hot blood of my slave ancestors coursing through my veins. And since for me, discretion was definitely not the better part of valor at that point, I let her have it. "Bitch, you're lying!" I screamed. That would have been bad enough, but I went further. I slapped her. She began shrieking, "Assault! Assault!" and grabbed a small wire container from her desk and threw it at me. Like a ninja in the movies, I caught the container, and threw it right back at her. Before I knew it, pictures and slides were flying everywhere! A catfight in an office—can you believe it! My beautiful new straw hat flew off my head as Judy ran out of her office screaming for help.

I picked up my hat, and my portfolio, and nonchalantly walked out of the office. I hadn't gotten far when her very effeminate assistant came after me, ranting that he had called the police and that I'd better stay where I was. I totally ignored him and calmly got in the first elevator that stopped at the floor. I didn't care if it was going up or down; fortunately it was going down. I got off at the next floor, put on my hat, quickly smoothed my outfit, changed elevators, and acted as calm as a cucumber.

When I got to the lobby, there was the assistant. He was so enraged, that he was practically foaming at the mouth, jumping up and down and screaming, "There she is! Guard! Somebody! Get her!" I walked serenely past the security guard and said, "I've never seen that man before in my life", as I threw my head back, walked out the door and hailed a taxi.

In retrospect, I'm certainly not proud of what I did, and the only explanation I can offer was, my relative youth, inexperience, frustration, and the sacrifice that I had made to come to New York. Also, as I said, having an Aries temper, I was used to giving people a piece of my mind, and just hated being lied to, and mistreated for no reason.

After the disastrous encounter at Judy's office, I was determined to make something better of the day, so I got out of the taxi and strolled over to the garment district, on Seventh

Avenue. Being brand new to the business and without any references, I made "cold calls", at several designers' offices in the area. Not surprisingly, I met with no success whatsoever. Feeling totally defeated, I went back to Paula's apartment and called my sister, Marian, "collect", to tell her what had happened. She laughed and thought I was very brave for standing up for myself the way I had. I wasn't so sure, and in fact, I spent the next few days on pins and needles, worried that the police would show up at the door any minute. They never did.

CHAPTER NINE

A Place of My Own

Thank heaven for my boyfriend Pierre. Soon, he found a tiny two-bedroom apartment for me, at 419 W. 119th St, Apt 9A, near Columbia University. The neighborhood bordered between upscale University students, and unsavory Harlem residents. The University area was relatively clean and safe. Three blocks uptown toward Harlem however, was very questionable, where as a woman you wouldn't want to be out on the street after dark. Still, I thanked God. I was grateful to have a place of my own, my very first apartment in New York that belonged to me, "be it ever so humble". There was an elderly doorman in my building who greeted me daily with a singsong quote "The Lady in 9A", which made me feel so special, and as if I belonged there. My sister Marian helped me furnish it with a complete new bedroom suite and often sent financial help as well, God bless her. When the energy is so positive and things run so smoothly, you just know you're in the right place at the right time. Now that I felt "official" I found a lawyer to legally change my name.

Over the next four months I knocked on the doors of what seemed like an endless number of modeling agencies, hoping for representation, and looking for work, trying not to succumb to living in "3D"—being depressed, disheartened, and dispirited. During my searching, I found myself being introduced to other models and different people in the industry. I slowly began to realize that part of the key to becoming successful, was getting to know and to be known, by the circle of people working inside the fashion industry. The same thing that made people successful in any field, NETWORKING. It seemed the more people I met, the more my social life blossomed. I was invited out all the time—to openings, discos, parties, receptions, and various other kinds of celebrations. Several designers who had not yet made a name for themselves became interested in hiring me, and I found myself doing shows in local clubs, churches, and hotels around the city, all of which kept me busy, kept my name circulating and thank God, brought in a little extra money. I would sneak into the back entrance of FIT (Fashion Institute of Technology) during the fashion show season, sit at the base of the runway, and watch models like Pat Cleveland swirling down the runway, and Billie Blair, floating so graciously. I would focus on their feet, and hands, figuring if I could get my feet to work like theirs, the rest of the body would follow. I later realized, everybody had their own style, and perfection, but boy did I learn a lot from watching them.

I had to take a temp job, via Clark Unlimited Personnel, (run by a savvy Black woman named Ruth Clark), sometimes to help supplement my income, however, my social life was booming. I found myself in the company of celebrities, rubbing elbows with the likes of Tamara Dobson, Melba Moore, George Benson, Walt Frazier, and top models Billie Blair, Alva Chinn, etc., Imagine! Me, Shailah Edmonds, hobnobbing with the glitterati! It was incredible. I went to so many affairs and high-end events and before long my picture began appearing in the society pages of local magazines and newspapers, one of which was Women's Wear Daily, the Bible of the fashion industry! One night I wore a black fitted crepe de chine dress, cut on the bias, with a white set in collar, which I found in a thrift store, with a pair of feathered earrings, which had a rhinestone in the middle. A few days later, my picture appeared in Women's Wear Daily, in Andre Leon Talley's Style Points section, in that dress, with the focus on the earring. Without realizing it, or even consciously trying, I had become the "it" girl, and doors started opening for me.

Two days after my photo appeared in WWD, I received a call from someone who introduced himself as Maning Obregon, a fashion illustrator for the New York Times. He had seen my picture in Women's Wear and asked, "Are you the model with the long neck, in a black dress with the feathered earring?" I anxiously replied, "Yes!" He wanted to see me as soon as possible. (I tell you, prayer works!) They say God watches over babies and fools. I'm not sure which category I fell into at this point, but Maning turned out to be another Godsend in my life.

A few days later I arrived at his apartment at 465 West End Avenue, and was greeted by his maid, Madame Bossier, and two small yapping dogs. I thought I had stumbled into a mansion. I had never seen such a sumptuous, spacious apartment. It seemed palatial—huge rooms with double height ceilings and French doors, furnished with the accoutrements of a life well lived; beautiful oriental carpets, and exquisite French provincial furniture. (I actually got lost a few times after using the restroom!) Suddenly Maning swept into the room; that's really the only way to describe it. He was a very elegant man from Manilla, Phillipines, and he was, what's the word that best describes him? Hmm, shall I say…Flamboyant? Yes, I can safely say that. He was dressed in a beautiful kimono and was naturally gregarious. I loved his personality immediately, and I guess the feeling was mutual, because he hired me right away, as one of his models. He complimented me on my appearance, said he loved my long neck, and snickered that anyone who could bitch-slap Judy Foster-Fell was a friend of his! (Turned out, he didn't have a very favorable opinion of her either). Well, I nearly gagged, but we became fast friends at that moment.

Maning explained that even though New York is the big city, it was a small village as far as the fashion industry is concerned, and that I was now becoming a part of that world, so I should be wary of my reputation. He had a stable of models that he referred to as his "children" that he hired constantly, and indicated he preferred everyone call him "Ma".

He worked from his apartment where clothes were sent from the most exclusive department stores; Bonwit Teller, B. Altman, Bergdorf Goodman, Saks Fifth Avenue, Bloomingdales, or whatever major department store he was featuring for the New York Times that week. Usually he would hire two to three models at a time and sometimes I worked alone with him. Rosalind Johnson, and Sherry Gordon were often hired with me and we would stand in poses for about ten minutes while he sketched us, (what an terribly talented artist he was!), and the drawings of us would appear in the New York Times within a week. Tommy Garrett was also a regular there at that time, and Maning would also set up photo shoots for us, invited us to lunch and dinner at his apartment countless of times, and boy did we have big fun!

He seemed to know everyone in the industry, and his designer friends would occasionally hire us for showroom work on Seventh Avenue. One day, he took all of his "children" shopping for designer shoes at The Chelsea Cobbler, one of the most exclusive shoe stores in the city at that time. "Child", Ma said, "if you're going to be a model, you'd better get used to wearing good comfortable shoes, cause you're going to be spending all your time on your feet; you'd better learn to treat your feet right". As I was soon to discover, truer words were never spoken. He bought us each two pair, and I'll never forget the feel of the buttery leather surrounding my feet, and the comfort of those shoes. Well, I was so proud of my first pairs of designer shoes, that each cost over $150 each, that I wore them for years, until they practically disintegrated. What a marvelous mentor, and great friend Maning turned out to be! I will never forget him.

At last, thank God, I was seen, and accepted by the Ford modeling agency, one of the most prestigious agencies in the business. The people there were very supportive, and sent me out on several "go-sees". I thought I was really special when the owner of the agency, Jerry Ford himself began to manage my bookings. I was called to meet him a few times in the office to discuss work, and on one visit, he asked if he could see me personally in my apartment. I flatly refused because he was married, but he assured me it would boost my career, so the naïve girl I was, conceded. On his visits, he told me his wife thought he was at his squash games, and I should never mention anything about these trysts to anyone. After the second visit, I realized there were no plans of me being on the cover of Vogue, or any viable career boost in the works, and these trysts were getting me nowhere, so I ended it. If any of his family questions this, don't even try it; I know where his birthmark was! (Yes the #Metoo was going on even then.) So be careful models, you never know whom to trust! After constantly pounding the pavement for hours daily going on go-sees, I landed progressively more prestigious jobs, one appearing as a model in the prestigious Bergdorf Goodman catalog! The most highly respected catalog in the industry at that time. All of it looked great on my track record, particularly at this stage of my career, but the jobs weren't steady enough to cover my bills. I was becoming discouraged again, and wondered if this was the right path for me.

As a new, aspiring model, I found myself testing, (taking practice shots), with different photographers, whose task it was to create different "looks" for me and help build my portfolio of pictures. One photographer took a great interest and genuine concern with my career. He was an Austrian, named Peter who spoke with a very heavy accent, and he was always very complimentary and particularly helpful. He made me feel so relaxed in front of the camera, and we'd always get great shots. One day during a photo shoot, he said to me, "You know dear, someone as beautiful as you should be working a lot more. You should go to Europe". It wasn't the first time I'd heard that from an industry professional, but each time I asked my agency about sending me there, they would say "it's not time yet" or, "no, you're not ready yet", or words to that effect. So I asked Peter where I should go? He insisted that there was only one place where I would start working immediately. Germany. Okay, I thought to myself, as I mulled over what he had said, then collected my belongings and left the studio. It certainly sounded like an interesting idea, but how could that happen. I was just a new girl trying to get established in New York.

Though no one in the industry was aware that I was a mother, every two weeks or whenever my budget would allow, I was in D.C visiting my children. They were growing fast, and what great times we had upon each visit. It was getting harder and harder to leave them, so I asked Leon if I could bring them to New York for a while. He refused, and that ruffled my Aries temper. He knew that if he gave me the children, he would sever any connection to me, but in hindsight, he was looking out for their best interest. Meanwhile, I was ready for a fight, so before I left D.C., I stopped by my old sitter Elaine's house. I told her how much I was missing my children, and I needed a plan to get them to New York with me. Being a mother, she totally understood my feelings, and agreed to help me. She called her friend Joyce, and we started the kidnapping plan. On my next visit to D.C, I was to rent a car, and Joyce was to be the getaway driver, while I snatched the children from their respective schools. We had to time it just right, so school would be ending, and I could get on the next air shuttle back to New York which ran every hour, (before the police was called).

For the next two weeks, I made plans to execute our plan. Everything worked like clockwork, I snatched the kids, Joyce drove the car and before I knew it, my children and me were on the plane back to New York, what excitement! Excitement my foot! Upon entering the tiny apartment, my oldest son Anthony, burst out in tears saying, he didn't like it here. The children hated New York, the small apartment, the busy streets, nowhere to play outside, but as children do, they soon adapted well. I got them enrolled into schools, and life was going OK, but bringing them to New York ended up being a huge mistake. It didn't take long to realize I could barely handle myself, and between work and socializing, I wasn't home often enough to give them the attention they deserved, and they were lonely and restless, a disaster waiting to happen. So after three or four months, I called Leon back sobbing, asking him to take them back. He agreed without missing a beat, and back to D.C they went. To this day I am so grateful to him, because if he'd refused, my career would've probably ended. (Leon passed away during the writing of this book) During that era, models that had children were considered old and used, so I had to keep them a secret for most of my career, as well as lie about my age. I read somewhere that your success depends on what you had to sacrifice to get it, and to me, this was the ultimate sacrifice.

About a week after our last test photography session, I went to see Peter to pick up my new photographs. He handed me my photos, and in a small envelope, something else as well. I opened the envelope and gasped. Peter had given me a one-way ticket to Frankfurt, Germany! I could scarcely believe my eyes. It seemed incredible that he could have that much faith in me, but, since he was such a good photographer and knew the business so well, I trusted his sound advice and judgment. It was then that I realized, because of the unbridled generosity of this man, that I needed to have the same faith in myself.

Peter had just finished a photo shoot, and a hairdresser in the studio overheard our conversation, and very flamboyantly suggested that if I was going to make a statement in Germany, I had to be different. He offered to do something dramatically different with my hair and I agreed. At that time I was pressing my hair with a hot comb, mostly wearing it in a chignon. After he washed my hair, it became a huge Afro. He then began shaping, fluffing and snipping, (a la Edward Scissorhands), until I ended up with an asymmetrical shape resembling a butterfly. Talk about dramatic! Peter was so inspired, and insisted on shooting me right away with this outrageous style. I thanked Peter profusely and left the studio with an extra spring in my step. Boy did the heads turn when I walked down the street!

Within a week, I picked up my new photos, and began packing and making arrangements to put my things in storage. I made plans to leave for Frankfurt the following week. It was incredible to me that my modeling career would get its real start in Europe, but who was I to stand in the way of progress! I was ready for whatever the old world had to offer a young, excited girl from the new world. Auf Wiedersehen!

Though I was getting around New York OK, I was still a naïve small-town girl. I was again swayed by fast talking guys, and my social life was somehow beginning to spiral, as I began partying with these high rolling, mafia guys. Though I knew they were dangerous, they were very protective of me, and I felt safe around them. Their financial generosity was spoiling me, along with the lush parties, and the drugs, (so much cocaine!) which thank God I only dabbled in very lightly, still only enjoying a puff of a joint now and then. I heard them planning things I can never repeat, and boy, did they throw me a lavish party before I left, which was the only time I felt I over indulged. My mind was in a haze when I arrived at the airport. I remember hanging on to the telephone (which was attached to the wall in those days), to stand up straight while waiting to board. I barely made it on the plane before passing out, and slept the entire flight. I was fortunate to get away from that crowd when I did, otherwise I knew I would've crashed and burned.

There is a sad sequel to this otherwise extraordinarily happy episode in my life, one, which I wish, were otherwise. Shortly before leaving for Europe, I received a call from Paula. It was clear from her conversation that she had become a full-fledged alcoholic by the slurring of her words, telling me she had been evicted from her apartment. I offered to have her come and stay with me for a few days until she could get organized; she arrived at my doorstep with all of her belongings in a shopping cart, and ten dollars in her pocket, very concerned that she hadn't had her hair done…strange. I let her live with me for a few days, until it became clear to me that she needed professional help, and more support than I could give her, so I called her father and asked him to come and get her. He eventually took her back to Portland, and I never heard from her again. Sometime later I heard she died under mysterious circumstances. Rest in peace, my dear friend.

Like Pip, the Dickens character from "Great Expectations", I could scarcely imagine what lay in store for me, but I had high hopes, and dreams of a new and better life in Europe. Little did I know how life-changing my sojourn in Europe was to be, how long I would remain there, and how it would become the scene of my greatest triumphs and joys.

Great, Great Grandmother Tillie ~ Former slave

Great Grandmother Clarise Lemonde Jones
Age 80 Born 1865, Mother of 7 boys, 5 girls

Great Grandmother Beaulah Johnson

Great Grandfather Mr Johnson (name unknown)

Grandmother Victoria Bivens

Grandfather Elmo Dave Jones

Grandmother Tecora Elaine Johnson

Grandfather Dock Robert Lyons Sr.

Grandmother Tecora was stylish and tough, and she could WALK!

Her Husband Dock Sr. was no slouch either

Mother, Myrtle Delores Jones

Father, Dock Robert Lyons, Jr.

Tecora, baby Me, and sister Carolyn

Tecora, Dad, Mother holding me sisters, L-R Marian and Carolyn

My first baby pose

My favorite picture at 6 years old

The Tween Years

Easter Sunday 15 years old

High School Years

14 years old   15 years old

16 years old   17 years old

I did my own hairstyle after my Mother spent hours doing press and curl

Easter Sunday, 18 years old with my son Anthony

L: cousin Brenda, R: friend Amber

Family Xmas L-R Carolyn, Mom, Dad, Marian, Douglas, me kneeling

 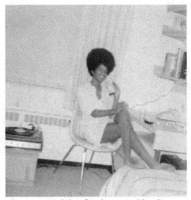

College days, notice the Colt 45 beer....the reason I didn't finish, partied hard!

Leon Edmonds — husband   KaRon — our son

Charles .P. Wood   on Break in C&P Lounge

Local shows -Washington. DC

Ruth Turner ~ my Mentor

First Cemetery Photo Shoot, Tombstones in background

WORLD MODELING ASSOCIATION COMPETITION 1975

Entry Ribbon

Prep with Jeanette Cooke

Composite/Model Award

The Coveted Trophy

ITS OFFICIAL...I'M A MODEL!

First NYC apartment — local work on wall

Becoming the "It" girl, socializing with celebrities, Tamara Dobson, Vy Higgensen, top models
Sheila Anderson, Alva Chinn, Billie Blair, Jennifer Brice, Marcia Tournier, and others. . . (photo Al Giles)

Andre Leon Talley's Style Points WWD 1975
The party that launched my career. Me with feathered earring (r) with celebrities Walt Frazier, Dick
Barnett of NY Knicks, Melba Moore, Vy Higgenson, Renauld White and more. (Lynn Karlin)

THE LAYERED LOOK

It's slim and it's in—the layered look. It's also one of the most comfortable. Tunics, turtlenecks, fitted skirts, pants, big sweaters and, of course, a scarf-shawl.

I'm afraid the prints haven't changed much for the winter, but you can create several different styles if you purchase ver-

LOOKING GOOD

satile basics such as those that can be worn with or without a belt, and/or has a split up the side or front. The best selection I've seen is at Macy's main floor, $25 to $35. Skirts and pants from $17 to $22 and big sweaters in the $40 range. I'd advise you to do some scouting before buying. There are several variations and price ranges to work with. The tunic can be worn with the skirt, pants or alone. You can put a turtleneck under it or a big sweater over it. For that "big bargain," don't forget to check out your favorite thrift shops.

Stovepipe boots look great, especially when the pants are inside and bloused over the boot tops. Top any of these fantastic looks off with a scarf that can also be worn as a shawl, wrapped once around the neck, letting it hang equally in front of you and behind.

While scouting I noticed some fantastic colors; rust/brown, burgundy and gray are the big ones. The materials are corduroy and tweed. However, if you want to get jazzy and do your number in suede, get Ultra-Suede, it's in.

With all these luscious layers there's no excuse for being cold this winter. Lay-er it on 'em, ladies!

—Shailah

Shailah is a free-lance writer and model based in New York City.

The mystical magical Maning Obregon

Model and Writer for Unique NY Magazine

THE BAGGY

A34-9A. The new jean star, the Baggy... becomes a new classic. Ours in blue cotton denim. Sizes 4-14. (2.25) A34-9B. Top it off with a padded-shoulder crew neck in white or currant red acrylic boucle. Sizes S, M, L. (2.25) The Sixth Sense

	Orig.	Now
A.	$36.00	$28.00
B.	$32.00	$24.00

THE WRAP-UP

A14-1A. Cuddle up to our thick cotton terry velour wrap robe. A classic by Royal Robes. In sherbert pink or chocolate. Sizes S, M, L. (2.25) At Home

Orig.	Now
$82.00	$48.00

Bergdorf's Catalog ~ My first major booking in New York

CHAPTER TEN

Sprechen Sie Deutsch? - Nein!

I landed in Frankfurt, Germany on a sunny, brisk November afternoon. After going through customs, and collecting my THREE huge suitcases, (I had yet to learn the cardinal rule of the modeling trade—to travel light); I strode out of the terminal, convinced that I was ready to take the modeling world by storm. I just knew everything would be fine, and it would be smooth sailing from now on, after all, I was in Europe now, ready for the big time! I hailed a taxi. "Please take me to a nice inexpensive hotel near the center of town" I asked in my most polite English. "Nicht verstehen" he replied. "Pardon?" I said in bewilderment. Then it dawned on me, he didn't speak a word of English, and I didn't speak a word of German. I was an American and naively thought everyone in the world spoke English! It never occurred to me that I was the one who should be able to converse in another language. After a few minutes of panic, I remembered I had been sensible enough to buy an English-German dictionary, which I had readily in my bag, so between that, some charades, and I'm sure some of the worst German this poor driver had ever heard, I somehow finally managed to find myself driving away from the Frankfurt airport.

It wasn't long before I arrived at a hotel in the middle of what looked like a pleasant residential district. I was so tired I just accepted it, thanked the driver paid my fare, and checked into the hotel—the person at the front desk was multilingual, thank God, so I had no trouble getting a room. The room was very clean, with a stereo radio, large fluffy pillows and blankets, and a funny looking old-fashioned phone. I guess I didn't realize how tired I was from all of the traveling, partying, and anxiety I had experienced, so after showering, I threw myself upon the bed, and fell fast asleep.

When I woke up, it was almost midnight. For an instant I was disoriented, and couldn't remember where I was. Oh that's right I was in Frankfurt. I turned on the radio, tuning back and forth on the dial looking for a station that spoke English, finally realizing there were none, and I couldn't understand one word they were speaking. After a moment of panic, I looked out of the window only to find it totally dark except for a few distant streetlights, but with the determination and absolute obliviousness to danger that can only come with youth, I made up my mind to take the bull by the horns and venture out into the nightlife. "Well Frankfurt, here I come", I said as I quickly dressed, had a bite to eat, and asked the hotel to call a taxi for me. This time I was lucky, the taxi driver spoke English, and I asked him to take me to the top disco nearby. He took me to a club filled with young people, all drinking beer and dancing. "Beer?' the waitress asked me. "Of course" I answered, either because I was intimidated by the fact that I didn't speak the language, or just wanted to fit in. (I'm not a beer drinker at all!). There were no Americans there, which didn't bother me, because being the only American, especially with my outrageous Afro hairstyle, made me the star. Finally someone in a heavy accented English, asked me to dance. Now that I understood! Apparently I made a good impression gyrating wildly on the floor, because other people came up to talk to me, and in a short time we became fast friends. We all left the club and went out to eat, and although I was somewhat bored, I made the most of the evening, found my way back to my hotel and fell asleep. Life was so much simpler and safer then. Although success requires some risk, I wouldn't recommend anyone to take such chances alone as I did then.

When I awoke the next morning, as I was washing and dressing, it really began to sink in; I was alone and ready to conquer Europe. While putting on my makeup, another reality hit me like a sledgehammer—I had exactly two thousand deutschmarks, (about $1000), at the International exchange rate. After doing a quick calculation of my hotel and expenses, it was clear to me that I had about two weeks before I could be homeless! I needed to find a job and fast.

I found a local phonebook and looked for a heading of modeling agencies. Fortunately, the English and German spellings were similar enough for me to figure it all out. I started with the one that had the boldest print, somehow imagining that the large print meant that it was the best agency. Unfortunately, no one spoke English; the same thing happened with the second call. The third time was the charm—someone spoke English, and asked me to come in at 2:00 that afternoon.

I found my way to the agency, and when I walked in with my huge, abstract Afro, all eyes turned to me in amazement. They obviously had never seen the likes of anything like me, and immediately went to find the one person who spoke English. She graciously told me Frankfurt was not the fashion capital, but Munich was the center for the fashion market, and that I should try my luck there. Somewhat crestfallen, but grateful for the direction and help, I went back to my hotel, packed my things and within the hour was in a taxi on my way to the train station heading for Munich.

My first impression of the train was very favorable. I was shown to a small, charming, clean comfy cubicle compartment with seats facing each other, (similar to, but a bit larger than a booth in a restaurant), with red velvety cushions. Each cubicle had its own door for privacy. The conductors would pass by, ringing soft bells, selling food from their carts, which made the ride quite enjoyable.

Upon arrival in Munich, I followed the same routine with my three heavy bags, but this time my taxi driver was very nice, and spoke English. Once again, God must have been watching over me, because not only did he speak English, but he also introduced himself, and asked me what I was doing in Munich. I explained my situation, and Wolfgang—that was his name—said that I could call on him if I needed any help. (Yet, another Godsend!) He drove me to an inexpensive hotel, which I again asked for, gave me his card, insisting that I not hesitate to call him. I thanked him, paid my fare and checked into the hotel, which was quite raunchy. The female manager was very masculine, and had horrible brown teeth when she smiled. Observing the people in the lobby soon led me to believe the hotel was in the equivalent of a "red-light" district, but since I didn't know where else to go, I was determined to try to make the best of it, at least for the time being.

By the time I got settled in my room, it was 5:00 P.M. on Friday, and all the agencies were closed, so I took a walk around the neighborhood, grabbed a bite to eat, and tried to acclimate myself to my new surroundings. Over the weekend I visited a variety of cafés and restaurants, and while there, met some interesting, helpful people who provided a welcome distraction. Who I really wanted to meet was someone who could give me some connections to the fashion community there—a booking!

First thing Monday morning I was back on the telephone calling modeling agencies. I made call after call and the result was always the same, either they didn't speak English or couldn't see me because I had no work visa. (Why hadn't someone explained to me that I needed a visa to work, or perhaps I should've done a little more research myself?) Again, I didn't want to succumb to living in "3-D, (depressed, disheartened, dispirited), but I could feel it coming on. Thank God, that afternoon Wolfgang rang my room and offered to take me out for a tour of the city, and to dinner. Afterwards, as I was getting out of the taxi, he handed me a newspaper saying there were ads for models in the back section. I spent the rest of the evening making lists of the agencies in the newspaper that I wanted to call, then decided to get a good night's sleep so I could get a fresh start in the morning. Modeling is a business!

I didn't have a telephone in my room in this dive of a hotel, so I went to the lobby to make phone calls. Once again someone saved me from myself! The front desk manager heard me making calls inquiring about modeling, and rushed over to me looking at the newspaper. He immediately told me to stop the calls at once. In only slightly accented English, he explained to me that the ads I was responding to, were for call girls and their agencies only. That Wolfgang! Wait until I get my hands on him. I was mortified and asked the manager for help. He couldn't have been more compassionate when he took the time to call the top agency in the city, International Talents Agency, and arranged an appointment for me the following morning.

My appointment was for 11:00 A.M, and I was on the dot. I was met by a gracious woman named Inga Schuckman, who explained to me that I could definitely work in the city, but I needed more photos (my tombstone pictures just weren't apropos) and what is known in the industry as a "zed card", a composite of 4 or 5 photos with my statistics, (height, dress, bust, shoe, waist, and hip size etc.), on the back, which she could organize for me, but it would take two to three weeks. I thanked her profusely, and accepted her kind offer.

I went for a long walk after my appointment, and as hard as I tried to be positive, I could feel a knot in my stomach. All I could think of, was how in the world I would make my money last two or three weeks with nothing coming in! I stopped on a park bench to look at my portfolio of pictures, I still thought they were very good (I still laugh at these pictures today!), and was confused as to why I needed new ones. I soon learned that photos that work for one market or country, (New York), didn't necessarily work for another. Every city or country has its own signature style, so following Inga's' instructions, I made arrangements for tests with different photographers Inga had recommended, to get the necessary photo's for my zed card.

When I returned to my hotel to relax I received a call from Wolfgang. I was still angry with him about the newspaper ads and let him have it. Despite my rage, he asked me out to dinner anyway, and I accepted. Considering my financial situation, it seemed foolish of me to refuse him. Over dinner I explained my financial dilemma to him, and he suggested I work in a bar until my modeling work began. I immediately told him I didn't come all the way to Europe to work in some bar, and I changed the subject. On the way back to my hotel, he sheepishly said he knew a man who ran a brothel in the suburbs. "How dare you!" I shouted, "What makes you think I want to be displayed like a common prostitute?" He simply shrugged and said, "Well you need money don't you?" I should've dropped him then and there. I can only say in my defense that it was indicative of how alone and vulnerable I felt at the time, and that I was grateful for anyone to take an interest in me and offer help. "I'll never be able to be a model if people found out." I insisted. He spoke to me as if I was a child, as if he were the voice of reason. "Just go and take a look at the place, maybe work for one or two nights just to get some cash, he replied." I'll just look," I said reluctantly, while pouting and arguing during the entire twenty-minute ride, about wasting my time with this venture. Right then and there it hit me; how vulnerable I was as a woman in a foreign country and how careful I had to be if I was going to survive. Over my years in the business, I've recognized that there are men like this on the sidelines everywhere, and whether you're a new or seasoned model, beware of these types. Be secure, confident and prepared!

I think it was partially to satisfy my own curiosity as much as to placate Wolfgang, I agreed to let him take me to the establishment. Finally, we approached a house with red lights in every window. My revulsion mounted every second. As we walked through the door, we were greeted by a man wearing very tight pants and high-heeled boots, who took one look at my boyish frame, (not a curve to be found anywhere)—and said he wouldn't hire me, because I was too flat. Thank God! In comparison with this joint, working at a bar all of a sudden didn't seem like such a bad idea.

After leaving, I asked Wolfgang to take me to his friends' bar, and while I waited in the car, he went in to ask about the possibility of work. While waiting, I noticed a well-dressed, intelligent looking man standing outside, seemingly lost in thought, because he didn't seem to notice me at all. When Wolfgang returned, I asked him to approach the man and ask if he wanted to meet me. "Wolfgang did as I asked, and lo and behold, he approached the car. I got out and Wolfgang introduced me to the gentleman who gave me a courtly bow and said his name was Alfred J. Linder, a movie producer. He gave me his card and asked me to call him in the morning. Before sleeping that night, I laid awake for some time thinking about this movie producer, what was he all about? What kind of movies? Still I made up my mind to take a chance and call him.

I woke very early the next morning, restless and very nervous, so I decided to go for a walk before meeting Mr. Linder. I passed by a strip club and, on a whim, walked in and looked around. (What an education I was getting!) A man approached me, and asked if I was looking for work and if I had a costume and a routine. I lied and shakily said yes, and he told me to come back at 9:00 that night to show him what I had, and sign a contract. I agreed, and headed off to Mr. Linder's office. To my enormous relief, Alfred seemed delighted to see me. After explaining my venture to Germany, I confided to him about my financial situation, and my need for immediate work. He listened carefully, and asked me where I was staying. When I told him, he was furious, and explained that it was a notorious place for hookers and their johns. Once again, I was totally humiliated, but Alfred was very kind, and accompanied me back to the hotel to get my luggage, and to help find another place for me to stay. I let him know how much I appreciated his help, (and that dreadful stripper joint was history!) as I realized Alfred had taken an interest in me.

Alfred took me to another hotel, which was very nice, clean, in a lovely neighborhood with lots of shops and stores, and near the subway. Over the next several days, he called and offered to take me to dinner. I gratefully accepted, and it was

Alfred who introduced me to the glories of Bavarian cuisine. While I was enjoying the meals and attention, I was uneasy about what he expected from me, but needless to worry, he was the perfect gentleman, never intimidating nor insisting on any "favors" in return. One thing did seem strange to me, however. During most of our dinners, he wouldn't eat, and when I questioned him about it, he would always say something about not being hungry. One day I unexpectedly dropped by his office to see how he was doing. He looked totally drained and after a few awkward, agonizing moments, he explained to me that he was going bankrupt. Oh my God! Here he was in major financial trouble, and yet so kindly buying my meals and looking out for my well-being. I gained even greater respect for him, and as my eyes filled with tears, I told him how much I appreciated his generosity and company, but I couldn't accept meals from him anymore.

During this time, I was testing with different photographers, getting my portfolio and zed card prepared. Money was going fast. I didn't hold anything back from Alfred at this point, telling him how desperate my financial situation was becoming. To his eternal credit, he was determined to try to help me any way he could. He found a chambermaid job for me at the nearby American Army base. I went for the interview, all the while appalled at the fact that I would be a maid in Europe. They hired me, printed an ID card, and told me I could start in the morning. Maybe I was somewhat spoiled when it came to labor, being that I had two older sisters who made it easy for me while growing up, or perhaps coming from an upper middle class neighborhood with a bit of education, whatever the reason, my pride just wouldn't let me take on the chambermaid job, and I can't believe I was so ungrateful as to never show up for work. Alfred was furious, and had some harsh words for me, but continued trying to find employment for me, finally referring me to the Munich Art Akadamie, to work as a nude model in an art class.

I was hired immediately, and for the first few weeks, the novelty of the job, being nude in front of a group of people, and considered a work of art, was quite fascinating, but after a while it became a bit boring, but at long last it offered me some honest money. I very quickly got used to being naked in front of a group of total strangers for three hours a stretch, (good training for my eventual modeling career, when you spend a great deal of time naked in a designers' atelier), and apparently the professor loved my poses, because he said that I was one of the best models he had ever had in his class.

The hotel where I was staying notified me that I would have to move, because my room was reserved for someone else in a few days. By this time I had put two of the suitcases in storage, and I moved yet again, this time to a hotel just three blocks away from Alfred's office. But even though I now had some money coming in, the hotel was still too expensive for my blood at that point, so that evening, I moved again to a pensione across town that Alfred found for me. He helped me with my luggage, and when we got to the room, which was large and clean, but somewhat desolate, Alfred became unexpectedly affectionate. It wasn't really something I wanted to do, but he had done so much for me, I felt I owed him something. We made love, or rather we had sex, and as he talked, I slowly began to realize that he was falling in love with me. The situation with him however, had unfortunately become untenable at this point, and I told him so. "Alfred" I said, "I'm not in love with you, and I don't think we should see each other anymore." He gathered his belongings, and after pleading with me to change my mind, finally left. But he wasn't quite finished, I heard him screaming from the street outside my window, "Are you sure, Shailah?" How sad. Finally, he left…So much for my prince charming.

By now, my portfolio and zed card were finished. I had gone to the Arbeitzamt and Kuntslerdienst to get my working visa in order, and Inga Schuckman said it was only a matter of time before I would be able to start modeling. I was so excited, and eventually quit my job at the University so I could go on castings. Inga proved to be as good as her word. Sure enough, after a few days of castings, she told me that a television producer wanted to meet with me. After so many false starts, dare I hope this could be the beginning of my modeling career?

CHAPTER ELEVEN

Europe Here I Come...Almost

I went to the casting with the television producer and was booked immediately. Finally, at long last, it seemed I was hitting my stride. Hallelujah! I was so excited; I was going to be on television for the first time, in a very popular German soap opera, Das Alter. The role I had to play was deceptively simple. I was required to be an elegant, impatient lady, waiting in a doctor's office. The few lines I was given in the script would be dubbed into German. Can you imagine me with my abstract Afro, speaking German! The shoot only lasted two days, but the pay was tremendous, more money than I had ever made in my life, in such a short amount of time! I was on a roll.

The television experience should have taught me something about money, and, in retrospect, it did, i.e., modeling work tended to be feast or famine: for a little while you're rolling in money, and then, nothing, at least for a while. But I had yet to learn to save for a rainy day. At the time, all I knew was, after a long period of having to watch every penny, the money I just made so quickly, was burning a hole in my pocket. Oh, and don't forget that I'm an Aries—we are impulsive and restless, always ready for a new adventure.

With no particular plan in mind, and for no particular reason whatsoever, I decided to take a trip. Can you believe it! I had lots of money, (or so I thought), and I wanted to do something different. I consulted my maps of various European cities, and decided, on a whim, to go to Berlin, where I heard there was lots of excitement and action. I was footloose and fancy free, so I bought a train ticket, and after what seemed a very long ride, arrived in the German capital. There were bright lights everywhere, and it all seemed very exciting and lively. I picked up a brochure that advertised accommodations, and I found a lovely hotel, and, true to form, after checking in, I decided to take a stroll around the city, even though it was late at night. I was charmed by what I saw; so much nightlife, and though I am the original night owl, I decided to turn in early so I could attend to business the next day.

I got a wonderful night's sleep, and in the morning decided to visit the modeling agencies, and television and film agencies, to see what work they could offer me. I struck out on all counts; they had nothing for me. The fashion industry was very small, and I was told the major fashion shows were held in Dusseldorf. Without speaking German, the television and film agents couldn't use me. I'd be lying if I said I wasn't disappointed, but I wasn't discouraged yet either. Back at the hotel I took out my trusty map, and decided to try my luck in Dusseldorf, where the notable fashion market industry was. I hopped on the train, and once I reached my destination, managed to see some agents. Although the agency representatives with whom I met were very nice, the fashion season, much to my chagrin had just ended and wouldn't resume until January, a few months away. Rats! I was beginning to learn yet another valuable lesson—timing is everything, (or nearly everything), in life. That, and the fact that all the clichés were coming true; you need to do your homework before making a major decision. And it helps to have a plan before you set out to do something as drastic as simply picking up and going to another city on a whim. What was that old saying—something about looking before you leap? Oh, well. I would learn that lesson later. Much later.

Back in Munich, the work was very slow, and since I wasn't doing as much work as I thought I should be, I decided to try my luck in Paris. Besides, even at this stage, I knew that Paris was the center of the fashion world, so off I went. Once again, however, I was my own worst enemy. Again, I hadn't planned for my visit to Paris, so things didn't go well. Firstly, I arrived at Paris Nord train station, a decidedly unglamorous section of the city, and everything seemed big, noisy, and confusing. Secondly, the hotel where I chose to stay, (found again by scanning brochures in the train station), was in Pigalle. Upon arrival there, I frowned at the thin, lumpy mattress, that had a few silvery bugs crawling on it, and I realized too late, what the area was known for; I was staying at the epicenter of the world's oldest profession, prostitution. And thirdly, I hadn't made any appointments of any kind. Despite this fact, I was anxious to see modeling agencies, so I hit the ground running; making the rounds to all the agencies, and every one of them turned me down. I returned to my hotel, disappointed and exhausted, and decided to treat myself to a nice dinner, and plan my next move. After dinner, the sun had gone down, and the neighborhood was totally changed, filled with noisy, sleazy night people crowding the streets. I was approached by a drunken man with a huge wad of francs in his hand asking me for a date. I refused and sped up my pace, as he began to follow me. By the time I got to my hotel, he was gaining on me, but I made it inside my room, located on the first floor, hastily slammed the door and locked it, as he was coming up the stairs. That flimsy lock meant nothing, because the man body-slammed himself against the door, and burst inside. As he stumbled toward me, he tripped on my suitcase, fell, hitting his head, and passed out, with wad of money still in hand. Frozen for a moment, I just stared at him, waiting for his next move, then decided he got what he deserved, and snatched the money. I grabbed my suitcase, which I hadn't even unpacked, walked casually out of the hotel, hailed a taxi and made my way to the train station. Suddenly, it dawned on me that maybe things weren't so bad in Munich after all, and that I needed to go back to where I got my first important modeling assignments. So, like a hurt puppy, off I went again, by train, back to Germany. Munich never looked so good!

CHAPTER TWELVE

Back to The Green Grass

S ure enough, my agent welcomed me back, and after I told her of my adventures, she realized she'd better keep me busy or she'd lose me, so fortuitously, and to keep me in one place, she immediately booked me for a month long tour of Germany, as a model for Wella hair products. Wow! This was my best booking yet, and the money was SWEET! It was funny; I couldn't get over the fact that my big sculpted Afro was such a huge hit, (that hairdresser in New York knew what he was doing). While on tour, wherever I appeared for a fashion shoot or runway appearance, people would come backstage and wait in line just to touch my hair— some of the towns I visited were very small, and I had to get used to people staring at me; I know it was only my imagination, but it seemed like even the dogs sometimes would stare at me! Still, I had no complaints whatsoever. Everyone was very respectful and treated me like a celebrity! I was grateful for the deference they showed me and thankful for such an amazingly pleasant booking.

After the tour was over, I was sitting in a trendy café in the Schwabing area of Munich, when a gentleman who introduced himself as a photographer approached me. His name was Cheyco Leidmann, and, I had no idea at the time, that he was one of the most popular working photographers in Munich. He was mesmerized by my hair and asked me if I had an agent, and when I gave him my agent's name, he set up a photographic appointment for me. After that photo shoot, and seemingly overnight, I found my face in every catalogue and fashion magazine in the city. He booked me for everything! They even put me, a black model, in every German ski magazine. Two of my favorite shots were when they put miniature skis in my Afro, as if they were going down slopes, and my first German cover, which was with a prominent Brazilian singer.

These were flush times for me financially, but just as important, I was learning what it felt like to be a busy, professional model. I was profoundly grateful for where my life seemed to be heading.

Things were looking up on the romantic front as well. I was out dancing one night when I met Paul, a gorgeous man from Poland, who, I later found out, was one of Germany's major soap opera stars. He recognized me from my appearance on Das Alter, and we began to see a lot of each other. We were photographed for society pages when we went out, became an item at social events, fell in love and eventually moved in together. Things seemed to be going well for a while, until I noticed that Paul had a problem. They say certain things follow certain people. It seemed that no matter what I did, I found myself involved with people who were alcoholics; my parents, my friends, you name it; (forgot to mention Charles had to join Alcoholics Anonymous toward the end of our relationship). I seemed to attract people who had problems with addictions. Perhaps I was so enthralled with the great time I was having I didn't notice the signs, but it seemed pathologic that I would once again find myself mixed up with an alcoholic. Eventually, apart from his jealousy, (he would always question if I was having affairs with other beautiful models and photographers I was working with), Paul became impossible to live with, mainly because his inability to control his drinking was getting worse. He began senseless conversations with himself or me, and could barely stand after a night out, to the point of embarrassment. I had to get away from him before I found myself slipping into the same state. During one of my fashion shoots, I met another photographer. His name was Stephan Krebs, and he had all of the qualities I was looking for—he had the four S's—sober, stable, sensible, and sensitive. He wasn't the fun, bad-boy type that I was usually wild about, but I decided I had had enough of that type for a while. Stephan had a huge apartment near the center of the city, and when I told him about the troublesome time I was having with Paul, he offered me his spare bedroom. He helped me move away from Paul, into his lovely expansive flat. Need I say my life in the spare bedroom didn't last long; we got along fine and enjoyed the time we spent together. He would take all the pictures I needed to add to my portfolio, and was also a great provider and a gentleman. Even my agent commented that Stephan was a good choice for me.

The fashion season was in full swing in Germany, and I was quite busy. I met several other models that I got along with very well who were going to model in Milan after the season was over in Munich. They didn't have to twist my arm or break my legs, to encourage me to join them. Besides, I had long been enamored of what little I knew about Italian style. Let's face it, the leather goods that were made there, were world famous for their quality, especially the shoes and handbags, which entailed exceptional craftsmanship, which I loved. I couldn't wait to indulge in this city. So, I told Stephan what I wanted to do, and that I needed to leave. He was very understanding, as always, even offering to let me store some of my luggage with him so I wouldn't have to pay for storage in Munich. By this time I had learned to travel light anyway. So, I packed my things and set off for Milan.

I checked into the Diana Hotel because I had learned from the savvy models that that was where all the top models stayed. I figured, a girl is known by the company she keeps, and I wanted to be considered one of them. I registered with an agency immediately, and was told that the runway shows were already booked, but that they would try to find some print work for me. The agency was as good as their word, and arranged bookings for me with Italian Harpers Bazaar, and other top magazines. I must say I fell in love with the energy and spirit of the Italian artisans I worked with. Suddenly, the Renaissance seemed to come alive, and I could really understand what it was like to live and work in the land that produced Michelangelo, Raphael, and Leonardo! The hair and makeup people were phenomenal. On one memorable shoot, they doused my hair with mud for an African effect. The set designers and other professionals actually built walls and painted them for each outfit I wore, to resemble whatever setting they wanted to create, and to accent every outfit I modeled. It was amazing. This whole period was a real whirlwind for me; I was dating and having fun, when I was suddenly called back to Munich for work, only to find when I got there that the job that they had lined up for me had been cancelled. That's the nature of this business! Not missing a beat, I made a U-turn back to Milan, but I found out that the season was over, and business would be slow until the fashion season began again in the fall. Like I said—feast or famine, and timing is everything!

Impatient Aries that I am, and since I once again had what I thought was a considerable bankroll, I decided, again on impulse, to head to Zurich, Switzerland, because I'd met some black models who were working there. Plus, the description and pictures that I saw on my maps and brochures were so enticing. But, once again, because I hadn't planned anything, upon arrival, I found out too late that the fashion season was very slow in that city, and work was minimal. To pacify myself, I treated myself to a great dinner near the hotel. As I was walking home, a handsome older man, blonde, very tan, dressed in all white, riding in a white convertible sports car, pulled along side me. He was very complimentary and asked if I wanted a ride home. I refused, and he slowly followed me to my hotel, while flirting with me. He asked to take me to dinner the next night, and after some hesitation, I finally accepted. He picked me up promptly, again dressed in his all white attire, and we had great laughs and conversation on the way. It was dusk, and the ride was getting longer, and the surroundings a bit more desolate. When I asked how far this restaurant was, he gave me a sneer and quickly turned off into a wooded area, and suddenly, only trees, with the sound of water nearby, surrounded me. He pushed me out of the car and took me to the edge of a cliff, and said if I didn't have sex with him in the car, he would throw me over. My heart was racing, as I stared at the swirling water nearly 100 feet below, and I concurred, as we trudged back thru the mud to his car. It had been raining and the ground was very soft. As we sat in the car, his beautiful white convertible began sinking into the mud. The wheels were nearly covered, and he began to panic and jumped out of the car, cursing. I jumped out at the same time, and ran as fast as these long legs had ever run in their lives, until I saw the city lights. Besides some harrowing plane rides, I had never, ever been so afraid. I was able to quickly hail a taxi back to my hotel. It was only by the grace of God that I survived this disaster, and needless to say, I was grateful, and learned a huge lesson. Frustrated at the thought of the money I had wasted taking this trip to Zurich, afraid this man was coming to find me at any time, I was in a sickening panic. Not wanting the front desk to see me leave, I climbed out of the window of my hotel in the middle of the night, without paying the hotel bill, and grabbed a taxi to the train station. I went back to Milan to get a plane to Germany, to the one place where I seemed to always find work—Munich. (The things we do when we're young!). I was taking airplanes like they were taxis. Seems every week or two, I was flying somewhere and this was only the beginning of my career.

Upon arrival in Munich, I moved back in with Stephan, contacted my agent, and again found myself doing all kinds of print and fashion work for months. Thank God for Germany. I did learn this time, to save a little of my growing bankroll and actually opened a healthy bank account in Munich.

On my next break from work though, the wanderlust set in again, and I set off for Rome, a city I had always wanted to visit. The architecture I saw in magazines left me breathless, and I'd heard the nightlife was amazing. Upon arrival in the city, sure enough, the architecture was breathtaking, and there was a certain smell of a damp basement that lingered around certain facades that really made you sense just how old and historic the city was. Just lovely to see, but doing business there is another story. Not only did I not find any work, but I also seemed to attract every scoundrel, and neer-do-well in Italy; one photographer I met, told me he was shooting a fashion spread in Milan in a few days and wanted to use me on the shoot. He asked me to meet him in the Hotel Diana in two days.

Naïve me headed back to Milan, and when I arrived I checked with registration to make sure the photographer was there, and left him a message asking for details of the shoot. He never returned my phone call so I thought I'd better get a good nights' sleep and be rested for the shoot the next morning. When I called him the next morning, he had checked out of the hotel. So much for the eternal city!

CHAPTER THIRTEEN

Paris Encore

Now that I actually had some real credits under my belt—beautiful tear sheets (photo spreads) from my appearances in International fashion magazines—I decided to give Paris another try. This time, I found a small agency that seemed interested in me, called Cosa Nostra, who sent me out on several castings. Although I was only hired for two shows for the upcoming season, I felt both discouraged and elated, all at the same time. It was my dream to be a working model in Paris, the center of the fashion world, but two bookings wouldn't give me enough money to eat and pay my hotel bill, and I refused to touch my savings in Munich. Once again, my contacts in Munich came to my rescue. I called a friend there who I remembered had mentioned he had friends in Paris, if I ever needed anything. I explained the extremity of my situation, and he gave me a few names to contact, that could possibly have some connections for work. (Always have a network of friends who can help you!). The old cliché of, "It's not what you know, but who you know", totally holds true in any facet of the entertainment business.

One of the contacts was with a journalist named Edit de Nicolay. She had connections with small, catalog-like magazines, where I did a series of "looks" for editorials. Kind of like the maid's work of print modeling. Magazines would use unknown models to create the style for the look they desired for the magazine, then call in the supermodel to shoot the real editorial spread. Between this freelance work and some other small shows I was able to line up for myself, I made enough money to live on. At this point, I knew in my bones, that Paris was both where I longed to be and where I belonged. There was a charm and a sophisticated attraction I truly loved, and could feel a great connection to. I just knew my future was here in this city.

The season in Paris ended successfully, and I couldn't wait to get back to America to tell the world I was a working model in Paris, and to see my children. I had been in constant telephone contact with them and was constantly picking up goodies for them along the way, even Italian shoes! I had refused to touch my savings in Munich so that I could share it with them upon my return.

I returned to Munich to see Stephan, retrieve my baggage from storage, and to get my money out of the bank. I adored Stephan, even though I was leaving him, gentleman that he was, he wished me well. He helped me pack my belongings— I had a lot of baggage, literally and figuratively by this point— and I found myself genuinely sorrowful to be leaving Germany, the place that gave me my start in the fashion business, and I will be eternally grateful to the German people for their kindness, patience and generosity.

Although I had grave misgivings about the wisdom of calling my former boyfriend Paul, to say goodbye to him as well, against my better judgment, I called him. We had experienced such great times and chemistry together. In a slur of words, he said he wanted to go with me to the train station— I was taking the train from Munich to Zurich, where I had booked an inexpensive flight back to the United States—and again, against my better judgment, I agreed to meet him.

When he entered the taxi, I could tell he'd been drinking, but I kept my peace. We loaded my bags into a luggage cart and settled into a cafe in the station. While waiting for my train, we decided to have a drink, and I began counting my bags, and suddenly realized one of my bags was missing. Just as I frantically began searching for it, thankfully, I heard the taxi driver calling out to me from a distance, in the station. He had found my bag in his taxi, and was running towards me to return it. I had so many bags I couldn't keep up with them! Between drinking and chatting, I didn't realize so much time had passed since we'd sat down. I happened to glance at my watch, and realized that my train was about to leave! I shouted the information to Paul, who by this time had become tipsy, (as usual) and he suddenly pulled out a ring and slurred a proposal of marriage. I quickly refused (in an "are you kidding?" kind of tone), as I started running, screaming for the train to wait as the doors were closing. Paul grabbed the overly stacked luggage cart and quickly ran after me. I jumped aboard, just as the train was starting to move, screaming for it to wait, but not before the cart with my luggage, slipped out of Paul's control, spilling my bags underneath the train. The train was unable to move. The bellman began waving his arms wildly as he blew his whistle loudly, and the train to come to a screeching halt, making an emergency stop. My bags were recovered, and we finally pulled out of the station late, which didn't sit too well with the passengers, who as German were sticklers for punctuality. Never has there been such a departure from a train station! What an extraordinary ending to a remarkable sojourn in Germany!

Leading the Wella hair show tour in Munich

German PlayBoy Magazine   Neue Revue Cover

SPORTIVE SKI MAGAZINES

Ski's in my 'Fro

(Cheyco Leidmann)

FIRST FITTING JOB FOR KAMAL, MUNICH, GERMANY. THE ELASTIC WAS TOO TIGHT!
(Stephan Krebs)

CHAPTER FOURTEEN

Unwelcome Home

Incredibly, it seemed impossible, but it had been one full year since I was in America, and my country seemed changed somehow, or maybe it was just me that had changed. Everything seemed familiar, yet strange. Upon my arrival to JFK airport, I pulled out my old trusty address book with names and telephone numbers of my friends, which after a few calls, I realized had gone out of date in the past year. Wow! I had no place to stay in New York! I had the good fortune of meeting a photographer on the flight who kindly offered to let me stay for the night at an unoccupied apartment belonging to his friend. After reaching the apartment, somehow it just didn't feel right, and I declined his offer. (Always follow your gut instinct!) I found a café nearby and kept trying to reach people I knew. Finally, as a last result, I found the number for my mafia friend. He luckily had found a new girlfriend, but was willing to help me. He knew an aspiring musician who lived in Greenwich Village, who was looking for a roommate. The song is really true—you got to have friends!

His name was Stuart Green, a very nice, and quite handsome Jewish boy, who held down a full time job, while pursuing a songwriting career in his spare time. Though he was a guitar playing songwriter, he was very introverted, and had no interest in show business or my life as an aspiring artist/model. We were cordial and respectful of one another, hung out a lot, hitting all the hot spots in the Village, had great times, but there were no bells and whistles when we attempted a romantic encounter, and we just weren't on the same wavelength career wise. While staying with him I used the time to make appointments to see every modeling agent in town again, and again was not only disappointed that I was turned down by them all, but also totally astonished by the way I was rejected by my own country. Can you imagine? Even with International tear sheets, (pictures from magazines), to show them, I was turned down flat for work in New York. And the excuses! That's what really hurt. I was told my European pictures weren't "American" enough by some. Others had the temerity to say the photos were great, but that they had their quota of black girls at that time. After the opportunities that had been presented to me in Europe, I wasn't prepared for the racism, and dismissive attitude in the country of my birth.

With no work ahead, I decided to call my old friend Maning Obregon, the illustrator from the New York Times. I explained to him that I couldn't find work, even with my freshly acquired European credits. Well, it seemed that my fabulous, flamboyant friend knew everyone. He informed me that it wasn't fashion season so there was very little going on in the showrooms, and the major shows were over. But he had a contact at the United Nations, with a client who was an African diplomat, named Dr. Hamza. He was in the oil business and was looking for a personal secretary for two weeks. Maning suggested I take it until I figured out my next move. God bless Maning! The job paid very well, and included room and board, (on East 62nd St. between Madison and Park Avenue), a very chic neighborhood indeed.Dr. Hamza was a nice man, tall dark and handsome, but very stern. Work and life with him was very hectic. My duties were to answer the phone, deliver messages, prepare breakfast, serve business guests, and prepare chicken EVERY night at eight for dinner, which I did diligently.

That seemed like the longest two weeks of my life, but I endured, and I didn't want to see chicken again for a very long time. The money was great, and when the job ended, I had plenty of money to visit and spoil my children. At the end of my last day of work, I took the next shuttle to DC, and spent the next two weeks with them. My, how they had grown, and initially we were like strangers. After movies, endless shopping, and fun outings, there were lots of hugs, and we were back in our comfort zone, sharing that wonderful, unconditional love, that only children can give. That seemed like the shortest two weeks of my life. It was very hard to leave them, and when I told them I wouldn't be back for a while, they understood and let me know that as long as I promised to bring gifts and money each time, it was OK. Kids are amazing.

Back in New York, I stayed with another friend, and decided to make one more final attempt to see every agent, photographer, producer and industry insider I could find. I scoured the city, but despite my best efforts, none of the people I contacted had much to offer. I considered going back to Paris, but even the cheapest flights were more than I could afford along with living expenses. So I took a chance and called Dr. Hamza, because I knew he had money to burn, to ask for an appointment to see him. Gentleman that he was, he agreed to meet me. I showed him my portfolio, tearfully told him about my children, and explained, imploring in my most convincing tone, that I desperately wanted to try my luck again in Paris. He listened patiently, and at the end of my recitation, told me that he was willing to buy an airline ticket for me, and put up some money for me to live on, until I found work. He then asked me to leave quickly, as his wife was on her way there from the airport. (Viva Africa!)

Within the week, I was on a flight headed back to Paris, but wiser this time, determined to make a go of it. I had learned through bitter experience that there was simply no substitute for drive, persistence and perseverance if you wanted to succeed as a model, or indeed, in any endeavor in life. I was determined to make a name for myself, to make money, and to fulfill the promise that I made when I won that haute couture trophy. There was only one place where haute couture flourished—Paris, and I was going to find my spot in haute couture, if it was the last thing I did in life.

CHAPTER FIFTEEN
Paris With A Vengeance

I t was October 1977, and I was in Paris again. It felt great
being back. Even though I arrived on the usual Parisian
overcast, cloudy morning, I maintained my feelings of
genuine love for this city; the enticing aroma of fresh croissants
in the morning, the topography of the city with its outdoor
cafés, the fresh haute cuisine, the art, the fabulous fashion of
course, and let's not forget the men.

My travels throughout Europe had given me a connoisseur's
appreciation for the God-given charms of continental males.
Though I loved the ruggedness of the German men, the beautiful
olive skin and dark features of the Italian men, there was
something special about French men. They were not especially
handsome, but had that certain "savoir faire", as they say. Just
in the way they carried themselves with confidence, their
elegant posture, and how they spoke with an eloquence that
never ceased to entice me, especially when they spoke English
with their accent, I'd just melt. They were natural gentlemen
with that indefinable quality that no one can confer upon you –
class. Most importantly, they knew how to treat a lady. French
men—bien sur!

I loved the language, which I picked up quite easily and
within a year, and without great effort, I was quite fluent in
French. Perhaps the fact (I later learned when researching my
family history), that I came from French ancestry, made me
adapt so well, and feel so comfortable there.

From the airport, I called the hotel where I had stayed on my earlier trip to Paris, and booked a room, but when I arrived at the hotel, the proprietor said there had been a mix up and he wouldn't have a room for me until the next day. "Oh, no, here we go again" I thought. By the expression on my face he knew I was just about to let him have it, and he offered me to stay at his apartment nearby. His family owned the hotel, and because of his responsibilities as the manager, he rarely stayed in his apartment. At that point I was so tired I would have slept in a hayloft, so I accepted his gracious offer, grabbed by bags and made my way to his apartment. Thank God I had learned to travel light.

The next morning, I moved into the Hotel Taranne at 153 Blvd. St. Germain, the epicenter of a very exclusive arrondissement (neighborhood), known as St. Germain des Pres. The hotel was just across from the Café des Flore where prominent artists and their contemporaries gathered daily. Tres chic! I went to my agency, Cosa Nostra, run by a very smooth talking Frenchman, Guy Heron who graciously greeted me and seemed genuinely glad to see me. Luckily for me, the Pret-a-Porter, (ready to wear), season was just shifting into high gear, and Guy gave me a list of designers who were having castings that I should visit immediately. Finally, my timing was just right! From my previous visit to Paris, I quickly learned that my signature sculpted Afro would not be acceptable for the French fashion houses which preferred a simple but elegant chignon, or a straight unfussy hairstyle.

So my first stop was to the hardware store to buy a hotplate for my straightening comb, which I had brought with me. Yes, I was staying on one of the grandest boulevards of Paris, in a refined hotel, doing my press and curl with Royal Crown hairdressing, on a hotplate! The first time I did my hair there, the manager, along with other hotel guests, came anxiously knocking on my door asking what that smell was. I explained the pressing process to them, and they soon got used to the smell of burning hair.

After getting my hair in order, I walked into the first casting and saw all the beautiful models there, and for a moment my heart sank. I remembered the words of my mother, and (as she had always instilled in me), held my head up as if I belonged there just as much as they did. After just a few castings, two things became clear to me; one, that I was somewhat taller than the other girls, and, two, and much more importantly, that I had a powerful ingredient. I had personality, with a capital "P"! As beautiful as many of the other girls were, they had a passive, blank appearance, and many of them seemed curiously listless. Not Shailah. No sir. I spoke with a smile and when a designer asked me to walk for him, I did what came naturally—refined by what Ruth Turner, had instilled in me from the beginning—I sashayed, I pranced, I strutted, I turned it out! Projecting your own distinctive style and personality is a huge part of this business and I learned early to have the confidence to do this, to be yourself.

If the designer liked the way you walked, they would ask you to try on a garment. Well! I was asked to try on garments by nearly every designer, because not only did I have a great walk, but I actually thought all of the designer creations I saw were just amazing, and they saw it in my facial expression. I loved and became a part of everything I tried on, which obviously showed on my face, and in my walk, (get it, aspiring models?), because by the end of the day when I checked back with the agency, I had been booked for three shows and had a few more weeks of castings to get more bookings. By the time I had finished going to all the casting calls, I was booked for nearly fifteen shows, and this was just the first season!

Make no mistake, though, it wasn't all a bed of roses. I realized very quickly that rejection was a big part of this business. On several go-see's, I was told "No", more times than I care to remember, and admonished by more than one designer, that I was too tall, I just wasn't their type, or that they had enough black girls, if they were using any at all. Enough black girls—can you believe it? I was really growing weary of hearing that phrase!

One casting I will never forget, during one particularly difficult day when I was very tired from going on dozens of castings, and the rejections. I was at the atelier of Guy Laroche, who tried to dismiss me as well, curtly telling me I was too tall for his collection. I'd had it, and before I knew it, a torrent of words came pouring out of my mouth, and I said adamantly "You know Monsieur, you need some tall girls in your show, they can show just as well as short girls and besides, it's boring to have all short models. Just let me try something on, and let me show you what I can"…I stopped suddenly when I saw the shocked look on his face. Apparently he'd never been spoken to in that manner, but must have sensed my frustration, determination, commitment and drive, and admitted that I was right. He then had a seamstress bring me out a colorful, harlequin print chiffon gown to try on, that flowed even as she carried it. As far as I was concerned, it was love at first sight between me, and that gown. Between the training from Ruth Turner, and Maning, the illustrator, (who had also taught me how to work a gown), and that "personality" thing I brought with me to everything, I wasn't holding back. Once I had that gown on, I walked and never stopped pivoting and swirling, until I was a blur of yards of multicolored chiffon! Monsieur Laroche was stunned and speechless. Needless to say he immediately booked me for his show, and not only that, my picture, wearing that very gown, made the cover of Time magazine at the end of the season! I had broken through the barriers and from that moment on, I never stopped working it.

"Civilians" think modeling is all fun and games and glamour. It's not. For one thing, you're on your feet all day. Second of all, you have to deal with hectic, chaotic days, which includes going for countless fittings, before the designers are ready to present their shows. While on the one hand, these fittings give you some "face" time with the designer where you can develop a personal relationship with him, on the other hand it is an extraordinarily tedious process. Time consuming as it always was, however, I always loved observing these masters of design at work. Dressmakers were summoned to make certain that your clothes were fitted perfectly, and various assistants made sure that you were properly accessorized with jewelry, handbag, hats, shoes, and whatever else the designer wanted as part of his signature "look". And with great pride and respect I came to understand, recognize and realize that I, as a model, was the designer's inspiration, both his muse and the one person who can transmit his idea of beauty and style to the world. I felt very privileged and very blessed to be a part of such a rarefied world.

Just to give you an idea of how hectic it could be; At the last possible moment, the designer might cast a critical eye over his creation, and suddenly be dissatisfied, and listening to some inner voice that only he could hear, would add or subtract a sleeve, lengthen or shorten a hem, or create an entirely new dress, right there, on the spot, many times just before the show! This is where a thick skin becomes important, because sometimes you were screamed at, ordered around, and even cancelled from a show at the last minute, if they found a model that suited the outfit better than you. There is major stress for everyone involved, (even the agents, whose models are being hired and fired constantly), until show time and you must learn not to take any of that personally, a very hard choice, but you must, for your own well-being.

Modeling for designers such as Yves St. Laurent, Hubert de Givenchy, Dior, Guy Laroche, Hanai Mori, astonishingly gifted and visionary designers all, I realized that by projecting my aura as a regal woman, I was a part of helping to bring something magnificently artistic to life, that I was the living vessel for the completion of these designers ideas of beauty, as they celebrated the female body.

About three days before the actual runway shows, the American "star" models would come to Paris for their fittings. They weren't required to go on castings, and occasionally I would do preliminary fittings for them, and when I saw one of them at a fitting, I was like a deer in headlights, in total awe. Pat Cleveland, Billie Blair, and the incomparable Iman were the top runway girls I admired during that time, and I would be walking the runway with them! I was so excited. Alva Chinn was also in the mix. I soon learned however, that my nice girl from Oregon personality that came to me naturally wouldn't fly here, not with these girls. During the shows, they would barely acknowledge your existence, and it seemed to me the better model you were, the less inclined they were to recognize you at all. I made the faux pas of saying something complimentary to one or more of them and they would condescendingly roll their eyes and smirk at me. Little did I realize that this was a very light dose of just how catty, and jealous models could be.

Well! In one of my first shows, I was lined up to walk the runway with two other seasoned American models, (who shall remain nameless), and just before we started to make our entrance, one of them turned to me and said cattily, "Do you really think you can keep up with us?" After my initial two-second shock and insult wore off, I snapped back at her, "I should think so, I'm taller than both of you." Meowww! The cat was in the house! From that moment on, I realized the cutthroat part of this business, and that this was war, and I was armed and ready. (No wonder Maning called makeup, war paint!) Darwin's theory of the "survival of the fittest" was most present right here in the modeling profession. But it was all good—the confrontation made me more determined than ever to show them that I belonged right up there, on the top tier with the best models in the business. Needless to say I not only kept up with them, I walked my ass off, swirling and posing harder than ever, getting applause with each and every appearance I made on the runway. I was triumphant. After the show, I couldn't resist looking down my nose, (along with a little neck roll), at the model that had been so rude to me, as if to say, you don't have any idea who you're dealing with!!

The next few weeks of fashion shows were so exciting, and fun. At that time, the trend was to have the latest disco music playing during the shows, and we kept up to the music while walking, swirling fabric, letting scarves float in the air behind us, slithering out of jackets giving major pizzazz and attitude, in the finest apparel that Europe had to offer. I thought I had the greatest job in the world, and by the third or fourth day, it all seemed like one big party, being recreated and pampered daily by incredibly talented hairstylists and makeup artists, cosseted by dressers, and designers who hovered and fussed over you before taking the stage. I would feel exhilarated and exalted knowing I was flawless from head to toe, and like matadors in the bull ring, I was engaged in a stylized battle with the other models to see who could get the most applause.

Growing up, I remember my Mother singing a rock and roll song by Lloyd Price called "Personality"—the lyrics said you were special because you walked, talked, smiled, charmed with personality; and it was really true in the world of the modeling. What a great feeling when you are the one, who can wake up the audience just by having enough confidence in yourself, to portray the attitude for the garment, simply by letting your personality shine through. You could actually feel it, the audience feeding off your energy, and giving it right back to you. Selling it!

When the season ended, there were fabulous parties that everyone in the fashion business attended. Top designers, agents and models were seen at the hottest clubs like The Palace, dancing to the sounds of the most renown DJ, Guy Cuevas, who had relocated from Club Sept, the other, now smaller, hot venue. I loved to dance, and found myself being the life of those parties, where I was noticed by, and met many new industry people by networking. I had made a name for myself and gained the respect, and perhaps the grudging admiration, of the top models in the business, who readily spoke to me with a smile at this point, and even showed even more respect when they realized I'd planned to live in Paris. They wondered how I just up and moved there without any direction. Courage, darlings, that's all.

I had only booked the hotel for three weeks, and one morning at breakfast, the owner told me the shocking news that my room was reserved for someone else in two days. By the look on my face, he sensed I was furious with him again, for promising my room to someone else without consulting me first, and you know my Aries mouth, I let him have it! We had developed a respectful friendship, and I could tell he was embarrassed, so he sheepishly told me there was a small room in the very top of the hotel usually reserved for maids. Since there was no twenty-four hour service in this small hotel, the room was never used and he offered it to me for as long as I wanted. It was small, but it had all the amenities and proved to be the perfect pied-a-terre I needed. I casually called it my penthouse and made it my residence for the next two years!

I have always been someone with lots of energy, drive and determination, continually on the lookout for new challenges and experiences. So after the fashion season, when a model friend asked me to join her dance class, I did so without hesitation. In retrospect, I don't remember what kind of dance or movement class it was, but I know I enjoyed it, and was good at it; so good, the dance instructor introduced me to a producer, who asked me to consider traveling with his dance troupe. After many rehearsals, the planned tour never materialized, nevertheless it was a great learning experience, toned my body and deepened my sense of my body moving through space, and enhanced my confidence. Essential qualities indeed for anyone interested in performing, and I highly recommend dance training to anyone aspiring to model.

One day after returning to my hotel from dance rehearsal, I received a strange telephone call, and little did I know how much it would change my life. The caller introduced himself as

Michael, and claimed he'd met me a year ago at a club in Paris. I assured him he had the wrong girl, because I was never in a club in Paris a year ago. He insisted on meeting me saying I would recognize him once I saw him, and imploring me to meet him, so I reluctantly invited him to join my girlfriend and I for dinner that evening. For safety sake, I would have never met him alone or in a desolate place. (I'd learned my lesson in that arena!)

When we arrived for our rendezvous, a short—he couldn't possibly have been more than five foot six—chubby man came rushing over and introduced himself as Michael. I was amused; he was obviously not someone I had ever seen before, and I found myself smiling at the idea that he might think he would ever have a chance of getting to first base with me. He turned out to be someone with a great sense of humor, and the three of us thoroughly enjoyed ourselves throughout dinner.

At the end of the evening, he invited us to a dinner party the following evening, hosted by a prominent art curator. We gladly accepted his offer. I decided to wear one of my best outfits to make a good impression; you never know whom you'll meet. I also decided to wear my highest heels and, because it was the weekend and I wasn't working, my huge sculpted Afro, so that I towered over Michael. I thought if I emphasized the disparity in our height, it would reinforce the idea that I wasn't interested in him as anyone other than a friend. As it happened, I needn't have bothered taking this precaution.

We were the first to arrive at an extraordinary residence at 54 rue du Docteur Luray. As I stood at the front door, I marveled at the workmanship. It was made of a fine stained wood and glass, and must have been twenty feet tall. We rang the doorbell and were greeted by someone I assumed, was the housekeeper. She was very cordial and ushered us into a magnificently appointed space that resembled an art museum, with African statues, artifacts, paintings, and object d'art from around the world, on display everywhere you looked. Eventually, our host arrived and speaking in a charmingly harsh but gentle voice, introduced himself as Jacques Kerchache. I wasn't the least bit interested in him and hobnobbed the night away with other guests. After a delicious meal, Jacques began to engage me in what developed into an intense discussion about black people; he revealed that he had lived in Africa for ten years and challenged me about our culture. He struck me as being over-confident, even arrogant, in his views, and, as a black woman, I challenged him point for point during our conversation. After a somewhat intense debate, we found ourselves in agreement about several things and before we knew it, were laughing heartily and truly enjoying each other's company. Ah! The "savoir faire" of French men.

I also noticed that, curiously enough, Michael had become interested in my girlfriend, and while they were obviously getting to know each other better, Jacques offered to show me the rest of the house, which had a beautiful decor, and the art objects were breathtaking, especially the collectors room which was he stated was off limits to everybody. After listening to his explanation of all the exquisite pieces, and absorbing all the history in that room, it was there that he caressed me, wooing me with his soft rough voice. And then he kissed me, and what a kiss it was. It was all so romantic. He then asked me to dinner the following evening, naturally I accepted, and from that moment on, we became an item; we were seen together everywhere, dinner parties, the opera, endless social gatherings…I was fascinated to learn about his life; he'd recently undergone surgery for throat cancer (hence, the rough voice), was an only child, and the woman, whom I assumed was the housekeeper, was in fact his mother; she often cooked wonderful meals for us, and his father was the caretaker of the house. I didn't know if I was falling in love with him, but I certainly knew that I had grown quite fond of him. He obviously felt it too, because after a very short time, he asked me to move in with him. I was in a dilemma, because, although I had strong feelings for Jacques, I also had my own career, and I instinctively knew myself well enough to know that I would get lazy, and begin to lose interest in it, if I agreed to live with him. I had sacrificed so much to get to this point in my life and I couldn't let anything compromise my progress. What tipped the balance in favor of my career was the fact that I had just begun doing fittings for Yves St. Laurent that week, arguably the most important haute couture designer in the world. I thanked Jacques profusely for his offer, but refused, and let him know that my career came first. Jacques couldn't believe it! I don't think anyone had ever rebuffed him before, and, because I seemed unattainable, it made him want me all the more. (Learn ladies!) Never was there a more determined suitor than Jacques; he spoiled me rotten, buying me jewelry, clothing, giving me money, whatever I wanted. He even sent me to his dentist for extensive cosmetic surgery to close all the spaces between my teeth. That Christmas, he gave me a gift that took my breath away—my first fur coat, from Revillion, no less! And what a great lover! He taught me how to fully enjoy the freedom of lovemaking. I can truly say I "grew up" in Paris. Yes, Jacques was one of a kind.

The moral of that story, boys and girls, is never turn down a legitimate invitation to go out, whether it be for drinks, dinner, or something else; you never know who you might meet or what might come of it!

CHAPTER SIXTEEN

Yves St. Laurent, Givenchy, Valentino, And the Rest of The Gang

T here are certain moments in life, which leaves one with an indelible impression. From the moment I set foot in the atelier of Yves St. Laurent, I felt I had entered into another realm. Everything about it was exquisite; it seemed to me to resemble an elegant theatre set, more than anything else. The gold-leaf provincial furniture was accented with red velvet cushions, like the interior of a jewel box. The decor was a backdrop for seamstresses and various assistants, bustling diligently but quietly about, tending to their creative duties. I approached the receptionist who smiled graciously and greeted me in a singsong way that I never tired of hearing in Paris: "Bon jour, mademoiselle". Once I had introduced myself to everyone, and became a regular there, I was always addressed as Mademoiselle Shailah, which made me feel even the more elegant. I was shown into the interior of the atelier, and, after slipping into an outfit that I was asked to try on, I suddenly found myself in the presence of the master himself. Yves St. Laurent, who, as far as I was concerned, was a legend, an idol and an icon, all rolled into one. I almost had to pinch myself to believe that I was actually standing right there, in his presence; it seemed quite surreal. This was the most renowned, revered, high fashion designer in the world, and, after hearing his name most of my life and seeing his clothing label everywhere, here he was, in the flesh. It was every models mission to show for this icon of fashion. The thrill for me was analogous to what it must be like for a simple Englishman to meet the Queen, or for a devout Catholic to be in the presence of the Pope. I actually felt a little light-headed, and realized it was because I forgot for a moment to breathe. I hoped that he could see in my eyes the esteem and admiration that I had for him and his creations. After being asked to demonstrate my walk, I moved with all the elegance, grace and style I could muster. He smiled and selected a few more outfits for me to try on. With each new garment, I became more relaxed and comfortable, and I was determined to give each article of clothing the treatment it deserved, by endowing it with a different personality. To my immense relief and joy, he said he loved what I did, and booked me for several fittings as well as for his next Paris couture showing!

Monsieur Laurent was very quiet when he worked, never speaking above a whisper when he gave directions to the seamstresses or talked to the models. His quiet demeanor had a calming effect on the entire atelier, and it was a pleasure to work in such a peaceful atmosphere. It rubbed off on me as well, and I found that I remained patient and quiet during the endless fittings required to create a garment.

Like every other business in the world, from high finance to accounting, it's a small fashion world, and everyone pretty much knew or heard of everyone else. Once word got around that I was Yves St. Laurent's fit model, all the other major designers were clamoring to book me for their shows. Suddenly, wonderfully, I was in demand, working again from sun up to sundown. I received booking offers from Dior, Guy Laroche, Elsa Schiaparelli, Hanae Mori, and Hubert de

Givenchy, Pierre Balmain, Claude Montana, Thierry Mugler, to name a few. At that time, Givenchy and St. Laurent were rivals--between them there was a relationship akin to the alleged rivalry of Bette Davis and Joan Crawford. It was an ironclad rule that anybody who worked for St. Laurent, could not work for Givenchy at the same time. Well, guess what black girl broke that rule first! That's right, I did it. And that, my children, is an irrefutable fact of fashion history.

Let me digress a moment, and speak about the travails of hair and make up for black models circa the late 1970's and 1980's in Paris. I was among the first wave of black models to live and work in Paris, in fact there were relatively few black people in Paris at that time, period. (I later learned of the Versailles models that broke the color barrier, but they didn't live there). Because we were still a rarity in the industry, hair and makeup artists in Europe were not used to applying their skills, or dealing with people of color. During my tenure with St. Laurent, I kept my hair straight, as I mentioned before, with the pressing comb, except for a few late nights with Jacques when I didn't have time to press it, I would grease my Afro so that it was slicked down on my head. (Alternately, the designer Schiaparelli loved my slicked down Afro, because it complimented the Egyptian feel of his collection). Black models had to either bring their own products, (i.e. perms, hair oils etc.) from the States, or hunt them down in the African neighborhoods, which was difficult and overpriced. It was totally by trial and error that the hairstylists finally learned to manage our hair.

Monsieur Alexandre was the premier hair stylist in the city at that time. He was in demand, and worked exclusively with the most prestigious fashion houses, at the request of the designers. If a hairstyle required a lot of work, I was sometimes sent to his beautiful salon on the rue du Faubourg St. Honore, an establishment frequented by the crème de la crème of Paris society. Sometimes I found myself amazed, a small town girl from Portland, to be in such exalted company. As it turned out, however, even the esteemed Monsieur Alexandre had a lot to learn about grooming for black women, as we were both soon to find out.

On this particular day, I arrived at his salon with a picture of the hairstyle that Monsieur St. Laurent wanted me to wear. I was already beginning to relax in the deluxe atmosphere, when I saw him reach for a spray bottle and began dousing my hair with water. I nearly jumped out of my chair! I patiently explained to him that water was not the way to slick back black hair. For those of you who don't know, allow me to set you "straight" right now; water is kryptonite to natural black hair—that's why, if you see a black woman who gets caught in the rain, or ventures too near a lawn sprinkler, she covers her head as best she can, and heads for the nearest shelter, away from the offending liquid.

Eventually, using gel and hairspray Monsieur Alexandre managed to create a masterpiece with curling irons. From a simple chignon or French twist to a major upsweep, it was pure heaven to get your hair styled by this genius of an artist. Your hair must be healthy, versatile, and manageable in this business, because each designer has different style requirements. For long hair, a good length is never past the armpits, because after that it interferes with the garment unless you keep it pulled back, or in a chignon. Today however, with all the weaves and add-ons, these rules are often broken.

Now let me touch on makeup issues during those times. Just as the stores and hairstylists were unfamiliar with the demands of black hair, makeup artists were totally clueless with respect to the makeup needs of women of color. Every woman knows that a perfect foundation is the key to being made up properly; the makeup artists in Paris knew that simple grooming rule as well, of course, but they inevitably never had the correct shade of foundation for us black models. They usually had to mix at least two or sometimes even three colors together to get anything even closely resembling a match for black skin tones, and even then the undertones of the cosmetics they used, left us looking ashy. Being that black people were sparse, the department stores didn't sell make up for us at all. Moreover, the makeup artists were particularly bad at highlighting our lips, going outside the natural lip line with color that wound up making us look totally "wrong". They were used to exaggerating the small lips of white models, not realizing most black people had full lips already. We politely sat through, what I'm sure they thought were their expert ministrations, and immediately headed to the ladies' room when they were finished, to correctly put our faces on. We relied on Fashion Fair cosmetics, or other ethnic products that we brought from the states to make sure that our foundation and powder, were as flawless as the rest of our hair and clothing.

Now, back to the runway. The fittings became really hectic the closer it got to show time. I must say that the fittings at times seemed endless, because, like all geniuses, St. Laurent was a perfectionist. He ripped a garment apart as often as he felt it was necessary, until he was satisfied that he had achieved his desired result. I never ceased to be in awe, as I watched an idea in pen and ink on the master's sketch pad, get transferred to simple muslin drapery, which in turn was transformed into a couture masterpiece in exquisite fabric, a process which, because every stitch was done by hand, required days, or more often weeks, of labor. And I always gasped with pure pleasure when I saw the finished product—another incredibly beautiful ensemble. Everyone worked long, hard hours, and we were all well paid. The atelier remained peaceful until shortly before the couture show was getting ready to be assembled; then, chaos reigned and, as the saying goes, all hell broke loose. It wasn't uncommon or unusual to watch a dressmaker putting the last stitches in a dress minutes before it was to be presented on the runway!

By show time, I felt I knew every dress in the collection, and to see them all lined up to be presented was just breathtaking. I watched Monsieur St. Laurent smile as he heard the thunderous applause that greeted every outfit as it emerged from backstage. Like the man, his shows were very grand, with an air of elegance and style. They were invariably held in the grand ballroom of one of Paris' most exclusive hotels, where the audience watched intensely from gold colored high back chairs, with those infamous red cushions. Needless to say, a veritable who's who of the fashion industry came to see each collection. Despite the festive atmosphere, when we hit the runway the models did not smile; showing the clothes was a serious, chic business, and it called for certain hauteur in its presentation. Only once, during one season, when I was showing a sporty daywear ensemble, (his first sportswear collection) however, I was asked to smile and do my fabulous swirling maneuver for which I was now renowned. I brought the house down and made the cover of Women's Wear Daily for the first time, wearing that outfit! Can you believe it!

Being a part of the couture shows always thrilled me, and I can distinctly remember sometimes putting myself into a self-induced trance, focusing on a particular place on a wall—"spotting" like dancers are trained to do—as I floated down the catwalk, pausing dramatically every now and again to strike an exaggerated pose, which I had planned, to accentuate the ensemble I was wearing. I hadn't won that haute couture trophy for nothing! I was totally in my element, and loved every second of the attention and applause that greeted my entrances, walks, and exits. Oh, let's face it, you have to be an exhibitionist in the best sense of the word to be a great model, and I, being the exhibitionist that I was, (and am), couldn't have been more pleased by the excitement that I was generating at the couture shows.

I had the utmost respect for this man, did I mention he was one of the first couturier's to employ black models, and because of his immense stature and prestige, was a catalyst for many of the other Parisian couture houses to open their doors to people of color? Bravo, Monsieur St. Laurent!

* * *

After the couture season, I received a call from my agent advising me that Monsieur St. Laurent was looking for a full time fit model for his cabine, (showroom), and that the master couturier would like me to come in to see him about the job.

The specifics of a full time fit model's duties, is someone who spends an entire working day, even during off-season, standing as a muse for the designer. The fit model is draped in muslin fabric to establish the idea of the creation, after which she is, (sometimes), sketched. The creation is then cut and pinned together, and brought in, in pieces, to try on the fit model, (and many times you get stuck!), making sure all the seams, fastenings, trimmings, lines, and structure are in place. The garment is then sewn, (for Couture, by hand!) and brought in for several final fittings. She also models in the showroom for buyers when they view the collection privately.

I told my agent that I was interested in the position, although deep inside I realized there were advantages and disadvantages involved in the arrangement. Of course, the position would mean more work, a lot more; I would be working eight, (or more) hours each day, five days a week, in the atelier, and I knew from past experience about my nomadic spirit, and the restless nature of my personality; I would chafe under those confining conditions! I didn't want to let Monsieur Laurent down, yet didn't want to tie myself down more than I thought was necessary. What to do?

Well, I was hired, and things were going smoothly, but as it so often happens at critical times in my life, my friend "fate" intervenes and decides my path for me.

This particular day, the fittings went on much longer than usual, maybe ten or twelve hours, because it was near show time. Normally during our fittings, there was always an assistant, or a seamstress, in the studio with us, literally at the master's elbow, awaiting whispered instructions. Uncharacteristically, at this fitting, I found myself alone with Monsieur St. Laurent while he was pinning me into a dress. Suddenly, without a word or warning, he crumpled to the floor at my feet. Was he unconscious? Had he fainted? I had no idea. All I knew was that I was in a state of panic, even shock. As difficult as it was for me to move with all the pins sticking out all over, and into me, I quickly bent down, shaking him gently, and calling his name. "Monsieur, are you all right?" Just as I was about to call for help, his assistant walked in and immediately started screaming for help, and screaming at me for not calling someone immediately. Weakly, I tried to explain that he just collapsed a second ago, but he didn't want to hear it, and asked me to leave for the day. I was shaking with anger and still in shock. I later discovered the dark secret of the House of St. Laurent—that the master, this indisputable genius, perhaps Paris's greatest couturier, had drug addiction issues.

Needless to say, I wasn't asked to work in the cabine anymore after the season ended. Shortly after, I heard he had hired a new girl named Mounia from Martinique. Mounia was only about 5'7" tall, and lacked the gazelle-like extremities that I had, but she became a top model over the years, and became Internationally famous from appearing in ads and showings for St. Laurent, all because she started out as a fit model for his cabine.

I, on the other hand was happy as a lark, because after the show season I did mini press shows for various designers in their ateliers, or various venues, print work for all the designers, and was hopping planes from job to job at venues all over Europe. Freedom! Though I wasn't Yves St. Laurents star, I was in my element and totally happy. One designer Phillipe Salvet took me on a six-day tour beginning in Cascais, Portugal where we did daily shows for the dignitaries throughout Europe. When traveling, all the models were dressed in white jumpsuits accented by pink model bags, while taking planes daily to places like Brussels, Lyon, Nice, and Zurich etc. How fab. Little did I realize at the time, that this was only the beginning of my fortune to see the world as a top model, places I'd never dreamed of seeing in my lifetime. The experience was exhilarating and exciting beyond belief. I'd truly become the "movin' star"!

CHAPTER SEVENTEEN

On A Roller Coaster Ride!

After a month of traveling, and mini shows, it was time for castings for the upcoming prêt a porter season, an exhausting ordeal of ten to twenty castings a day, for two weeks. By this time I was familiar with the routine and took it in stride, beating those streets like nobody's business. Since I was always looking for a challenge, during that busy time, I even decided to join the American Church in Paris where I took voice lessons and sang in the choir on weekends. The choir director Jim was very funny and flamboyant. I learned a lot musically, and boy did we have some laughs.

After the castings in Paris, my agent Guy Heron, took me to Milan, Italy for the shows there, that preceded the Parisian shows. I signed with a top agency there called "Why Not", headed by a wonderful lady named Tiziana Casali. No sooner had my flight landed than it seemed that I was off to a round of castings and fittings, though since I was a proven high-fashion model from Paris, there were more fittings than castings, because I was booked before I even arrived!

What an amazing success it was for me in Milan. I averaged about seven or eight shows a day for my first season, working for top designers including Armani, Versace, Missoni, Mario Valentino, and Fendi among others. It was a whirlwind blur of a week.

A typical day began with an arrival time of 7:30 AM, for preparation for a 10AM show. Next an 11:30 show, a 1PM show, a 2:30 arrival for a 4 PM show, a 5:00 arrival for a 7 PM show, dinner, ending with a 10:00 PM fitting for a show the next morning, with a 7:30 AM arrival time. Between the fashion shows, late night fittings, fabulous dinners, parties peopled by the most gorgeous men imaginable, I barely remember sleeping at all. Though there are glamorous aspects to the fashion business, it's physically demanding, hectic, and a lot of hard work. This is the reason it helps to be young, and physically fit to be a top model.

When the last show ended in Milan, I flew back to Paris immediately, to begin the shows there. Suddenly, I realized there were more Black models than ever in Paris. They had become the rage! It seemed that any black girl who'd ever thought about modeling could find work there, but would've never been given the opportunity in America. There were also many ex-pats, models who had made Paris their new home, not only from America, but Africa and the Caribbean as well, including Gloria Burgess, Kathy Belmont, Mounia, Sherry Gordon, Rosalind Johnson, Carol Miles to name a few. Now my name was added to that list, though my stay only lasted a bit over two years. Givenchy had an entire cabine (showroom) of black models who were also expats, including, Lynn Watts, Sandi Bass, Patti Arrington, twins, Donna and Danita Johnson, and Diane Washington. Milan, Italy also had their crew of expats including Geneva Hutton, Valerie Davis, Paulette James (Armani's muse), Vody Najac, Kim Clark and Romney Russo who also shared her home base in Germany.

Several major Parisian designers used black models as muses in their atelier. After being on the Time magazine cover for Guy Laroche, I had become his muse (yes, the one who told me no!). The French recognized this, and we were all photographed for a prominent French magazine, which is featured in this book. You couldn't go to a major designer's show without seeing several black girls on the catwalk strutting their stuff! Jan Maiden, Tanya Dennis, Aria, Charissa Craig, Jamie Foster, Olivia Chapman, Gail Quarles also did very well there during my time and a bit later, CoCo Mitchell, Lu Sierra, and Roshumba Williams to name a few. Most of us, being from a background of seamstresses or stylish people from church, brought reality, a real love and style to the clothing. We had never been dressed in such finery! I gave thanks that I had been among the first to break the color barrier, and had helped open the door to make it possible for other girls to make it in this business. I was also proud of the fact that the fashion press, for the first time was exposed to a host of black models in all their diversity of hair texture, skin tone and black beauty. We were a rarity for the French, a novelty, bringing all of our southern mannerisms, and church upbringing to their culture, which they loved and responded in kind, treating us like royalty. What a season! What a time to be alive and working in Paris!

The first thing I did upon returning to Paris was to call Jacques to tell him of my success in Milan. He was overjoyed to hear from me and invited me to dinner, where he listened patiently to my tales, but didn't seem to respond with the enthusiasm that I expected. I was soon to find out why.

After dinner, Jacques told me he'd received an assignment that required him to travel for three months. He gave me the ultimatum, to either take a break from my career to travel with him, or we'd have to break up. I was devastated. What was I to do? He was asking me to make a terrible choice; either give up my career, even temporarily, at the peak of my success, or say goodbye to a man that I had genuinely grown to love. How could he ask this of me? I'd sacrificed so much and worked so hard to get to this point, I was in my prime, how could I stop now? I tried to explain my dilemma to him, but to no avail. I realized, and so did he, that he was the type of man that needed someone by his side, a companion, or a lover, who could give him more time and attention than I had to offer. Heartsick and in tears, I told him that I couldn't give up my career, that I had to keep moving forward, and if that was unacceptable to him, that we would have to end our relationship. As we kissed goodbye, I felt something go out of me, and I was filled with indelible sadness. Jacques promised to keep in touch, and I told him that I would collect my belongings from his apartment at some point. C'est la vie.

Thank God, during this desolate time, fate stepped into my life once again. The next day when I went to my agency to check in, among the designers I found out that I'd been booked for, was the masterful Valentino Garavani, another major icon in the fashion industry. I knew then, that I had made the right decision about Jacques. As my agent ran down the list of other designers I was booked for, I began slowly sounding out the names and addresses, writing them slowly, when my agent actually snatched my appointment book from me, and wrote the names for me, because I wasn't writing my bookings fast enough! He said I'd never make my fittings writing at that speed! I had a show for Lanvin at 11AM, Valentino at 2:00, Michel Goma at 3:00, Tan Guidecelli at 4:00, Sonia Rykiel at 5:30, and Jap at 8PM! It went on like this for a full week. My relationship had ended, but I had more shows than I'd ever done, and finally ascended to that rarefied realm where I had become one of Paris' most sought-after models. Ne pas regret rein!

PRINT MILAN, ITALY

MIGUEL CRUZ   GEORGIO ARMANI

WALTER ALBINI   MISSONI
(photo: Maria Vittoria Corradi)

129

FENDI LEATHER TUNIC   FENDI RECORD DRESS
(Photo: Cristina Ghergo)

With Geneva Hutton, Kirat (L),
Billie Blair (R) Missoni family (L)

PHOTOGRAPHED BY ANDY WARHOL AT "AREA" CLUB,
FEATURED IN ITALIAN VOGUE

With Gloria Burgess

ROME, ITALY

SHOWS MILAN, ITALY

(Also pictured Alva Chinn, Jerry Hall)

Miguel Cruz 1981

Krizia show, with Beverly Johnson and Gloria Burgess

With Billie Blair

AND JUST A FEW MORE…..

Most photos: Graziano Ferrari)

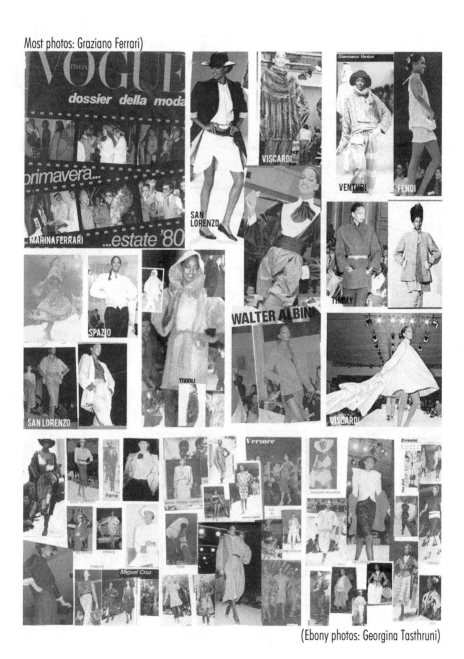

(Ebony photos: Georgina Tasthruni)

VALENTINO COUTURE SHOWS ~ ROME

VALENTINO

Photos: Arthur Elgort   With Kathy Belmont and Sandi Bass

FINAL COUTURE SHOW ~ ROME – 2003

Outside at night with 100 Prancing Stallions and Natalie Cole opened the show
(Photo: Rino, Rome)

With Pat Cleveland and Natalie Cole

Wild Child to Couture Style

CHAPTER EIGHTEEN

The International Crown

After an amazing season of prêt-a-porter shows in Paris, I had a wonderful, long, sought after affirmation, of my success as a top model. So immersed was I in the excitement of the season, and basking in the afterglow of walking the runway for the biggest names in the industry, I scarcely gave my home country a second thought, and certainly had no immediate plans to return to America anytime soon. But once again fate, the spirits, destiny, or call it what you will, interceded and pushed me in a direction, to make a decision, which I otherwise would not have made.

A Japanese woman by the name of Hanae Mori was one of the world's most important designers at this time. Although her headquarters was in Tokyo, she also maintained ateliers in Paris and New York. Because my agent had a hunch that we might work well together, one day he arranged a casting for me with her at her studio. How right he was! Upon meeting her, I thought she was one of the most beautiful, elegant ladies I'd ever met and, to my utter astonishment, I was later to discover that she had a gorgeous son, who I fell in love with at first sight. As much as I flirted with him, he totally blew me off, but I secretly kept my mad crush on him, as did all of the models!

Anyway...I thought Hanae Mori's designs were exquisite, and she felt that the special style I brought to the runway, a mixture of elegance, combined with my signature swirling technique, was perfectly suited to showing her creations to their best advantage. We developed a wonderful rapport, which resulted in me being booked for every runway showing she had. My photo was featured on a poster for Elle magazine, wearing her design.

During the busy season, sometimes the shows would run late, causing me to be late for my next show, but she, among other top designers I modeled for, (Armani, Versace, Givenchy, Dior...), would not start their show until I arrived, keeping key press attendees and buyers waiting. That's star power, darlings! From the Phillipe Salvet tour, and this experience, I realized that designers like to work with a proven winner, and once they recognize you can "sell" their garments, they insist on using you every time they possibly can. I recently learned from an agent, that sometimes customers would buy a garment before seeing it, simply because it was worn by a certain model. I reiterate, it's all about "selling" that garment!

After one show, Madame Hanae, as she was called, approached me about a huge presentation she was planning in of all places, Minneapolis, Minnesota. Who knew there was a huge Japanese population there? She thought it would be wonderful if I would come along to model in the Midwest engagement, and thereafter do small shows for her in New York as well. As she explained the details of the presentation to me, I was struck by the fact that this major booking was scheduled for my birthday. I, again, took it as a sign, and interpreted this serendipitous turn of events as a favorable omen. What better day was there to lay legitimate claim to my title as an International high-fashion model, than to return to the states in triumph, from my victories in the fashion capitals of Europe? I quietly thanked God for this major opportunity, and told her I would be honored to join her. The staff of her atelier made all the necessary travel arrangements. We were to fly to New York, stay for a day, then on to Minneapolis. When we arrived in New York, I checked into the Barbizon Hotel for Women on 63rd Street and Lexington Avenue. I had heard about the Barbizon before. It was safe, convenient, and comfortable, if a little bit dreary. I had only planned to stay for a few weeks, but, as it turned out, this unlikely venue was to be my home for the next two months! Hanae Mori had a vocal, passionate and well informed following in the United States. The models that I found myself working with in Minnesota were very cordial and treated me as something of a celebrity, because I had worked the runways in Paris. The show was a great success, and I was proud to be a part of it. (She took me and a few other models, to Mexico City a few months later, where we did a show at the estate of the late Barbara Hutton).

Back in New York, one of the first calls I made was to the Ford agency, to let them know I was back in town, and available for work. I just knew that with my recent string of European engagements, and with new tear sheets and photos in hand, they would be clamoring to use me as well. Wrong again. Despite my obvious talent and experience, they were nonplussed. They replied somewhat unenthusiastically, asking me to drop by when I could. Not exactly the ringing endorsement I had hoped for, or frankly thought I had earned at this stage of my career, but not so surprising when put in the context of the time. The year was 1979, and during that time, there were "print" models, (mostly white), that appeared in all the top magazines, (Vogue, Harper's Bazaar, etc.) with photographic layouts, to appeal to the readers and buyers in the Midwest and Southern states. And then there were the show models, (mostly black), that worked the runway shows, did showroom modeling, and weren't as visable to the general public. The Ford agency however, was nice enough to refer me to their sub agent, Ellen Harth, a very savvy woman who handled their models for the runway shows, and who also kept up with the modeling scene in Europe. I was very pleasantly surprised when I called her. Ellen was genuinely ecstatic to hear from me and asked me to come in right away. Again, timing is everything, (well, almost everything), in life. The show season was just beginning in New York, and Ellen started sending me out on castings right away. I think Hanae Mori somehow had the foresight to know that the time was right for me to make some additional inroads in the fashion world in New York City, and I will be forever grateful to her for taking me along with her, and giving me the opportunity to prove myself in the Big Apple.

Within a few days, I was booked for Bill Blass, Stephen Burrows in Bendels, Anne Klein, Versace and Yves St. Laurent shows among others, while still doing the Hanae Mori mini-shows in between. It was an amazingly productive, but hectic period, and I found myself scheduled for many additional shows even after the formal season ended, work that gave me a steady income for the next two months, (that's why I extended my stay at the Barbizon). I was even able to hop on the shuttle to Washington, D.C. on many weekends, to see my children. I was FINALLY accepted in the New York fashion world, a place I had struggled to be for years. Life was grand.

Early Paris casting, Portfolio in hands, Press and curl hair
(Jane Thorvaldson)

FIRST CIGARETTE AD ∼PARIS
(PhilipeMonnier)

PARIS PRINT

L'OFFICIEL MAGAZINE (Christina Ghergo)

*metro*Madeleine
scènes furtives des dessous Parisiens

photos.Uwe ORmer illustrations.Patrick Taeron
style : GENEVIÈVE VIAL
coiffeur : YANNICK pour HARLOW maquilleur : RAMON

ELLE MAGAZINE

143

COUTURE SHOWS PARIS ~ PARIS

YVES ST.LAURENT

PIERRE BALMAIN   DIOR
(Laurent Durand) Coiffure: Alexandre de Paris

144

COUTURE AND PRET A PORTER ~ PARIS

AFRICAN AMERICAN MUSES ~ PARIS 1980'S

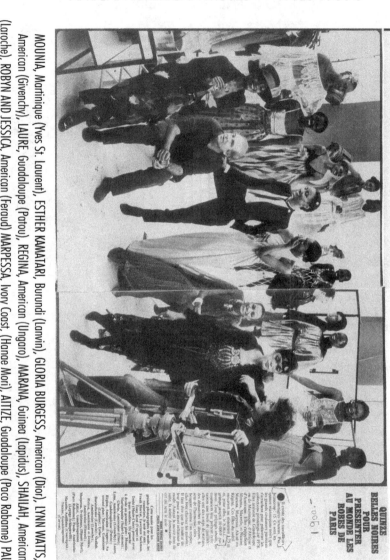

MOUNIA, Martinique (Yves St. Laurent), ESTHER KAMATARI, Burundi (Lanvin), GLORIA BURGESS, American (Dior), LYNN WATTS, American (Givenchy), LAURE, Guadaloupe (Patou), REGINA, American (Ungaro), MARANA, Guinea (Lapidus), SHAILAH, American (Laroche), ROBYN AND JESSICA, American (Feraud) MARPESSA, Ivory Coast, (Hanae Mori), AITIZE, Guadaloupe (Paco Rabanne) PAULA, American, (Lepage-Schiaparelli, MAXETTE, Antilles (Courreges), NICAISE, Guadaloupe, (Carven).

During my early years in Paris, I was whisked off to Abidjan, Cote D'Ivoire, (Ivory Coast), West Africa. They worked me! I did a full day photo shoot, radio, and a fashion show. I don't' remember the money being that great, but there is no amount great enough to pay for the opportunity to experience Africa. I stayed in the Hotel Ivoire, but had the chance to spend the night with a family and experience the food and culture. What a life changing experience. I would encourage anyone to visit, especially African-American people.

ABIDJAN ~ IVORY COAST ~ WEST AFRICA

(Photos: Philippe Monnier)

Then Finland!

147

MADRID, SPAIN

Where I met German makeup artist Alexander Becker, who helped secure this shoot for me. We still remain friends.

GRECO MAGAZINE

Mili Carrasco

Pilar Rodero

Photos: Gema L. Fernandez

CHAPTER NINETEEN

Music and Fashion - My Passion

ear the end of June, on one of my many shuttles to Washington, D.C., I met an entertainment lawyer named Milton Rothman, who represented, among other artists, Betty Wright, (singer of the hit song "Clean Up Woman"). Betty was managed by Danny Sims, currently the husband of Beverly Johnson, who was the top Black print model in the country at the time, in a field dominated by white models. How incredible was it that I met, apparently by the sheerest coincidence, someone connected to other people who shared both of my most passionate interests—music and fashion. I told Milton of my love for music, and how I wrote poetry and songs, in my spare time. "You know", he said, "Betty is working on her new album, and would probably welcome some new material, why not look them up? Tell them I sent you." As he gave me his card and their contact information, I was stunned; could this be yet another wonderful coincidence in my life?

A few days later I found myself being announced to the Sims residence, by the doorman at 1215 5th Avenue. I tried to be as nonchalant as possible when I entered the sprawling Fifth Avenue apartment, and was introduced to Beverly Johnson, and her family. Was it just a figment of my admittedly overactive imagination, or did Beverly seem to give me a desultory glance when I was introduced to her? I know it sounds petty, but in the ultra-competitive world of modeling, we girls are always sizing up the competition. And, truth be told, even though I hadn't been a working model as long as she had, I had nevertheless achieved a level of success in an area of the business, (the runway), in which she couldn't compete, and I was both taller and thinner than she was to boot. Consciously or otherwise, I think she might have been a little resentful.

Even though Beverly was a little wary, I kept my composure as I was introduced to the other people in the room, including Kevin Kendrick, Betty Wright's keyboard player. Kevin was very nice to me but more importantly, was a phenomenally talented musician. To this day I have rarely heard anyone match his talent. We jammed together for the next several days, playing around with different lyrics and melodies, and soon came up with some great songs, one of which Betty Wright loved called, "Listen to the Music". It was actually being considered to be the hit of the album! The chemistry between Kevin, who was a 19-year-old virgin, and I, couldn't have been better. We began having fun trysts, even though I was ten years his senior. What he taught me musically, I taught him sexually, and no pun intended, but we made beautiful music together in both genres. Both Kevin and Betty wanted me stay and continue working, but I had received a call from my modeling agent. It was July, the couture season was beginning in Paris, and I was wanted for the runway shows. Reluctantly, I left without signing anything, promising to contact them when I returned. I was so jazzed. It seemed that the spirit was with me no matter what I became involved with, and although I was on my way back to Europe to live out yet another chapter in the fashion world that I had come to cherish, I could also look back on a very special experience with two wonderful musicians. Yes, thank you, God. Life was good.

Before I left New York, I realized I had to do something about my insatiable sex drive. I literally had no time to date, or have a relationship during fashion season, and since breaking up with Jacques, nothing was happening in Europe, so I made a trip downtown to Greenwich Village, and picked myself up a nice vibrator with a universal adaptor.

July 2, I arrived in Paris on an uncharacteristically beautiful sunny morning, eager to start my second couture season. Castings had not yet begun, so I settled into my "penthouse" pied a terre on Boulevard St. Germain, and took some time to enjoy the city for a week, discovering new arrondissements, outdoor cafés, museums…What a treat to marvel at all the wonders of the City of Lights, and realize I was a part of it all—it was heavenly.

My relaxing reverie was abruptly interrupted when I got a call from my agent to say I had to begin castings. I could scarcely catch my breath before I was caught up in a whirlwind of castings, making my rounds all over the city at lightning speed. Fortunately, most of the designers knew me by now, and welcomed me back to do their shows, and the new clients were equally receptive. How great it felt to be finally known, recognized, desired and respected in the industry. Just a few short seasons before, I was being told "no" incessantly, and having to prove myself to those responsible for booking models. Now, top designers wanted me, Shailah Edmonds in their shows. Perseverance pays, darlings!

The Paris season was a resounding success for me, so much so that I was invited to Rome thereafter for their Couture season, working for Tivioli, Barocco, Lancetti, and of course Valentino, among others.

Signore Valentino had always been kind to me, and it was a joy to be able to work with this great master of design again. One night the fittings at Valentino went well into the night, and the couturier, the perfectionist that he was, asked me to raise my arms for what seemed like the 100th time to make yet another miniscule adjustment on a dress! Being young and impatient, I scrunched my face in a clear expression of annoyance, and the photographer, Arthur Elgort took a memorable photo of me at that moment. Imagine me, being impatient with a renowned couturier! We laughed at that for months.

July is very hot in Rome. Many hotels and ateliers didn't have air conditioning, and we were showing winter couture, which included fur and fur- trimmed garments. It was a condition you just had to accept, but at times, backstage was literally unbearable, and we were sweating bullets. But once onstage, the element of performance dissolved any discomfort.

There is no better fit in the world than in a couture garment. Every seam in the garment is manipulated to fit every nook and cranny of your body, allowing you total ease, comfort and movement, and the feeling of being completely pulled together. It is totally my element, and I worked it, making more money than I had the previous couture season. I was also able to enjoy some of the sights of the eternal city including being wined and dined by the beautiful men, and enjoying irresistible food. I absolutely loved it, and had many wonderful summer nights there. One night, back in my hotel, I was exhausted and incredibly horny, so I decided to try my new vibrator, which I never had time to try before now. I took a hot bath and got comfortable, plugged it in, and got in position to do my thing. When I turned it on, I saw a spark fly, heard a loud buzz of electricity, and all the lights went out. Five minutes later the manager of the hotel was banging on my door, asking if I had done anything with electricity, because the entire hotel was without power. Of course I lied and said no, and when he left, I buried the vibrator deep into the lining of my suitcase as I laughed silently, but uncontrollably. Damn! I had blown the electricity in the entire hotel, and never got to use the vibrator! Boy, was I glad to see everything restored the next morning. I am so glad to write this book to tell this, because at that time I couldn't tell anyone. What a hoot!

Back in Paris, show season was completed successfully, and I was totally exhausted. Most Europeans take the month of August for vacation. The majority of fashion houses, and businesses are closed for the month, leaving mostly tourists attractions open. I decided I had earned a vacation as well, so I made arrangements to fly back to New York. I boarded the plane with French Francs hidden in my shoes, under my arms, and any other creative place I could hide my money. At that time, the Franc was worth much more than the dollar so I was faring pretty well. When I landed, I called Ellen Harth to tell her I was booking out for a few weeks. "Oh no you're not!" Ellen shot back. "The cruise season is just starting here, let me make a few calls." God bless Ellen, she called me back to let me know that she had me booked for a full week of shows!

Upon completing my shows, I decided to check in with Kevin Kendrick, Betty Wrights' keyboard player with whom I had written songs, to see what was happening on the music scene. Well, it's a good thing I did. Kevin told me the album was finished and Betty had recorded one of our songs "Listen To The Music" for her album "Travelin' In The Wright Circles"! Not only that, she was performing it at the Apollo theater the following night, opening for Bob Marley! I was elated, until I met Kevin the next day and saw the album. I checked the back of the album, and the album itself, for my co-writing credit, but it was nowhere to be found. I had not been given any song-writing credit whatsoever! Welcome to the music business! My heart sank, and I was fuming. I asked Kevin why he didn't include me, and he just gave me a confused look. I certainly wasn't going to take this lying down. Immediately I called Milton Rothman, the lawyer that introduced me to Betty, who got back to me, and within a few days had reached an agreement with her. Though my name wasn't on the album, I was added to the recording contract and would receive royalties accordingly, which in fact I did for several years thereafter. Though that severed my ties with that operation, I will never forget the joy, and humble feeling that I had when I heard my lyrics live, on stage, at the notorious, Apollo Theater; what a blessing. Nevertheless, I learned an invaluable lesson; friendship and having fun is one thing, but business is another. In any creative endeavor, modeling or any of the performing arts, you must have a written, signed agreement specifying your duties, and how you are to be compensated for it. To any aspiring models or creative types, please know that all the handshakes and verbal agreements in the world can't make up for a legally recognized document, with signatures of all the parties involved. For the rest of my career, I never forgot that valuable lesson.

CHAPTER TWENTY

Family Reunion Whirlwind

After so much time working, I finally had a break, and decided it was high time for a family reunion. I made plans for a whirlwind family tour. I picked up my children and took them to Portland, Oregon to see their grandparents, then to Seaside beach resort, and on to Mt. Hood ski resort. We then boarded a train and took a scenic ride down the West coastline to San Francisco, to see the children's Aunt Marian, my sister. The last leg of the trip was to Shreveport, Louisiana to see my grandmother—their great-grandmother whom they had never seen. I hadn't seen her myself since I was a child. Needless to say, the reunion was a treat for us all.

Back in New York, I received a call from my agent to say that the most important department stores in the city, Bergdorf Goodman, Bloomingdales, Bonwit Teller, and Saks Fifth Avenue, were featuring shows by European designers. I barely had time to make appointments with my hairdresser and manicurist, before I was booked for the likes of Armani, Claude Montana, Guy Laroche, Givenchy, Fendi,Versace... The following week, the stores featured American designers, and I found myself working for Bill Blass, Mary McFadden, WilliWear and more, after which Guy Laroche flew me to Toronto for a major show.

The summer seemed to go by in a flash, and, with the approach of September, I had to head back to Paris for the prêt a porter shows. Before the shows even began, I was whisked off to Rome by the Fendi sisters, who requested my participation in a special fashion show they were having. (No, I didn't take a vibrator; that was the end of that!) My agent suggested I go to Milan from there, because the shows were starting in Milan in two days. In Milan I was booked for eighteen shows a day, (my record there was 22 shows a day, each show with different hair and makeup!). There was no time to think about anything, just like a trained thoroughbred, get out on the track, (runway) do the shows, follow your schedule, and try to get rest and eat whenever you can. The glamorous world of modeling is first and foremost, tough, demanding, and exacting work. Drink lots of water!!!!

During this season, the Italian models were furious that we were taking all their work away from them. Little did we American models know that we didn't have the proper working visa, so the Italian models promptly notified the police of that fact. Our agents warned us not to answer questions from the police and to avoid them by any means necessary. For about three or four days, the police were waiting outside our shows to arrest us. We would have the playboys waiting in their cars at secret doors, to whisk us away immediately. A few times I missed a car, and found myself running like crazy after a show, and once even hurdled a fence! Slowly the danger began to wane as the police got scarcer, and we managed to finish the season under less duress. The following season, we arrived with proper visas.

After Milan, three things happened in quick succession that let me know I was at the top of my game. I returned to Paris, where I did exceptional work with the most important designers. Then it was back to New York for another round of appearances in a phenomenal season. But the epitome of success was when I received an invitation from Hanae Mori to appear in her shows in Tokyo, Japan. It was incredible. I had conquered New York, the capitals of Europe, and now, the jewel in my crown, Japan. And it wasn't going to stop there! I had truly become an International high fashion model!

CHAPTER TWENTY-ONE

Travels and Travails

After flying for nearly 20 hours, I arrived in Tokyo, Japan. From the time I descended the plane, as weary and jetlagged as I was, I marveled at that city. The people were extremely courteous, and after I retrieved my luggage, I walked out to the curb, and stepped into a taxi whose doors opened and closed automatically – imagine! The city was immaculately clean and very much like New York City, but on an even more intense scale, the city glittered with endless neon lights and signs, none of which I could read.

Madame Hanae, as always, had seen to every detail, to assure that our stay was as pleasant and comfortable as possible. We were assigned translators, and chaperones, which accompanied us everywhere, until we were secure in our hotel rooms, which put a damper on my spirit of adventure, but I was kept so busy, that I didn't miss it. My hotel was the Nikko, the premier hotel at the time, in the center of the city. Upon entering my room, I noticed a beautiful floral arrangement waiting for me with a welcoming note from Hanae Mori. The amenities at this top-flight hotel were both charming and addictive, including the comfy complimentary kimono-styled robes, nightly bed prep, and incredible massages for a very nominal fee.

The theme of the fashion presentation was "Tokyo 6" featuring Hanae Mori's top six favorite designers from her favorite cities, Jean Muir, Thierry Mugler; Paris, Issey Miyake; Tokyo, Gianni Versace; Italy, Stephen Burrows; New York, and herself. Other designers Zandra Rhodes; London, Kansai Yamamoto; Tokyo and Sonia Rykiel showed as well.She also booked her favorite models including Pat Cleveland, Martin Snaric, Gloria Burgess, Susan Hess, Vody, Aria, and myself, among others. She had even arranged for the Soul Train Dancers to perform! What a lady. The entire affair was gloriously enjoyable from beginning to end, and at the after-party, designers, models, and dancers all drank sake until we were thoroughly looped, but the most unforgettably, fabulous, fun time was had by all.

My dear friend and fellow model, Jane Thorvaldson, found an agent for me in Tokyo, who invited me back to do shows there. I worked there two seasons, living there for three months at a time. Boy did I eat a lot of rice, but like in other cities, models were always invited out to eat or ate free in most restaurants. On one occasion, I was asked to return, and at that point only had my youngest son KaRon living with me. Without missing a beat, I bolted upstairs to my neighbors Jeanette and Fred Tinsley's apartment, which I would often visit. I actually asked them to watch my son for a few months, as if it were a few hours, while I whisk off to Tokyo. Jeanette and Fred Tinsley, southern folk with huge hearts, were so proud of my career and readily accepted. I will be forever grateful for them for that huge favor.

During one season in Tokyo, an American rap group called Wild Style, fronted by Grand Master Caz, came to perform there. They were creating quite a buzz, and all of the models planned to attend the concert. They were amazing and the crowd went wild. After the show, I went backstage to meet them, and they were just as excited to see another black American as I was, and invited me out to eat. Well Grand

Master Caz himself took a liking to me, and after LOTS of sake, invited me back to his hotel room. We were having a ball, lots of laughs and began to get romantic. When I laid down next to him on the bed, all I remember saying was "Uh-oh" as I felt my stomach churning, and vomit slowly rising up to my throat. It just wouldn't stop, and like a mighty fountain, I heaved all over the bed, made a trail to the bathroom and it ended there. As I put my face on the cold toilet for comfort, I could hear the Grand Master calling housekeeping, and asking to change rooms. Luckily, I was still dressed, cleaned myself up as best I could, and slurred, "I have to go", and darted out of the door. Every time I look at my autographed picture of him, I laugh. Maybe that was God's way of protecting me again, but it was a night we both will never forget! Wild Style!

After Tokyo, over the next few years, I found myself literally traveling all over the world to appear in fashion shows. My normal routine was Milan, Florence, London, Paris, New York, along with surprising places like Genoa, Italy, (home of Christopher Columbus), Madrid, Spain, Helsinki, Finland, and Abidjan, Africa among other places. I saw so much of the world it was mind-boggling!

On one of my trips back to New York during fashion season, I'd grown tired of the drab green walls of the Barbizon hotel, and realized it was time to find an apartment of my own. To be ahead of the crowd, every morning at 6:30 AM, I was at the nearby newsstand to purchase the New York Times, to peruse the real estate ads. After a week or so of contacting landlords, I was shown several lovely places, but they were in parts of the city totally surrounded by concrete, glass and steel. Being from Portland, I was used to being surrounded by trees, and grass, elements of the natural world, and if I was to stay in New York permanently, I was determined to live in sight of the same. Finally, my wish came true. I found a listing for a two-bedroom apartment on one of the most prestigious streets of New York, Central Park West for $550 a month! I visited the apartment, and although I didn't have a park view, it was spacious enough, had lots of closet space, and with the park just across the street, it spelled happiness. I signed the lease immediately, although I had no time to buy furniture or furnishings, because I was traveling shortly, but again, I had a place of my own in the city. With only a mattress on the floor, and clothes in the closet for the first year, I gave thanks for my new apartment, loved the location, and have kept this ever so humble abode to this day.

A few days later, I decided to relax, and take a bus ride, instead of the subway, to my appointment, something I'd rarely done, because the slow buses do not lend themselves to my fast paced lifestyle. The bus stopped just in front of my building, and after boarding and finding the perfect window seat, I noticed, there happened to be a neighborhood paper called Our Town on the seat next to me, which I picked up. Thumbing through it, I saw an ad in the classified section listing a furnished, summer bungalow in the Catskills for sale, with an asking price that actually fit my budget; $9,000. I was very attracted to the idea, because ever since my affair with Jacques in Paris, who had a summer home that we visited often on weekends, I learned, among other things, that the only way to survive the stress, hustle and bustle of a major city, was to have a hideaway in the country. A place to rest; where the beauty of quiet and nature could surround one. I had promised myself that someday I would have a country house, so the next day, I took a ride upstate to see the bungalow, and fell in love with it at first sight. As the bus stopped adjacent to small plaza that included a gas station, a post office and a general store, the driver announced Spring Glen, my stop. After debarking, I turned around in a complete circle, admiring landscape. It reminded me of Portland, with mountains on every side, fresh air, and acres of trees. I walked about 200 feet to Kraw St, and entered the grounds of the bungalows. I met the real estate owner, Joel Efrein, who gave me a tour of his newly acquired property. All of the 20 co-op bungalows were vacant, meaning I had first choice of any one I wanted! The fenced grounds were spacious and beautiful, surrounded by trees and there was even a pool on the grounds, which the tenants would share. I chose a two-bedroom bungalow, just in the center of the property, far enough away from the pool to avoid noise and people. Again, love at first sight! I wasn't going to let this opportunity pass me by, so I signed the stock certificate right away, promising to pay in cash the following day, and got the bus back to the city. Tomorrow couldn't come fast enough; I was so elated and smiled the entire way, as I drove a rented car back to Spring Glen. I paid for the property in cash, and that modest bungalow became my sanctuary that I treasured for many years. I called it my "Sanity Palace", because it gave me the balance I needed to survive the travails of living in the fast-paced city of New York, and my hectic life in general. After a whirlwind-buying trip in New York to furnish it, and my New York apartment, it was back to Italy for the shows.

My mother had the opportunity to visit my bungalow during her one visit to New York, and was so proud of my success, though after a day, she was bored stiff. She wanted to see the city. When my children joined me in New York, we enjoyed many wonderful summers there. I was totally in love with life.

TOKYO PRINT

Left Collage; Issey Miyake Party Me Singing with Pat Cleveland and Vody
Right Callage: Candid Pics of The Best Six and The Soul Train Dancers

Rap Group Wild Style   Autograph By Grand Master Caz

ther smashing success

rsen. Fred Miyake, mannequin Shailah, Yuya and
ager nequin Erika.

That gorgeous black girl on
the runway is **Shailah**. She's
new in Tokyo, comes from the
Big Apple and is something
very special.

SHOWS TOKYO

LONDON PRINT

BRITISH VOGUE

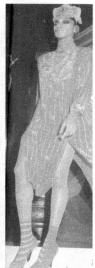

ZANDRA RHODES

LONDON SHOWS

ZANDRA RHODES SHOWS WERE PURE DRAMA WITH IMPECCABLE DETAIL...

AND SO MUCH FUN!

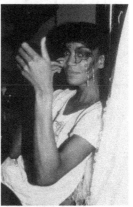

Flew the Concorde jet to Zandra's show, NY to London in THREE hours

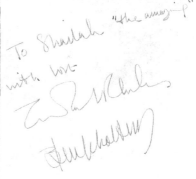

Zandra personally thanked me with postcards for each show, and autographed her book

Zandra in center, her assistant Ben, and her cluster of models

Silk evening breeches with quilted jacket, right, by Janice Wainwright. Pirate suit by Vivienne Westwood in striped cotton, below right. Ballgown by Bruce Oldfield in snake print with sequins, below center.

Arabella Pollen   Janice Wainwright

I am acutely aware of my spirituality, and very connected with the "unseen" world in which we live, somewhat of a mystic I suppose. As a child, as I mentioned earlier, when I went into those trances, (staring into space and dreaming), I felt as if I was closely connected to a spiritual world. It was mid-March of 1981 during the prêt a porter shows in Milan, when I had one of the numerous encounters of this kind. I was on the runway during a Fendi show when suddenly, inexplicably, I was overcome by a wave of emotion; a strange feeling of incredible sadness. Despite the glamorous fur, the accolades from the audience, the fabulous hair and make-up, that usually rouse me, did nothing for this overwhelming unhappiness I was feeling. I couldn't shake it. Was it ennui or torpor I was feeling? Had I become bored or jaded with the entire fashion scene already? I couldn't really say, all I know was that my spirit was troubled, and I wasn't surprised when the show was over, when one of the Fendi sisters noticed the change from my usual exuberant energy, and said "Sheela, why you look so sad?" After all, I was known for my flash and dazzle, my spirited stage presence, pizzazz and ebullience. I couldn't respond. I just wanted to be alone, and after my day of shows were completed, I headed back to my hotel room. No sooner had I sat down to unwind, the telephone rang. It was Tiziana, my agent, telling me to come to the agency right away. I asked her if it could wait until tomorrow, but she insisted that I come right away. Oh, God, no rest for the weary, I thought as I headed out to hail a taxi.

When I arrived, Tiziana had an unfamiliar look on her face. I couldn't imagine what was so urgent, or why she looked the way she did. She sat me down and, and I managed to ask her "Tiziana, what's so urgent, why do you need to. . ." She cut me off as she poured a glass of straight whiskey. This was very odd, and I questioned, why and why now? She just adamantly said "Just drink it, drink it all." I was about to say that I didn't want a drink, certainly not now, but I had always respected Tiziana, and we had many fun times together, so I put the glass to my lips, and drank. Before I could get the last swallow down, she looked directly at me, and told me that she had received a call from my sister, Marian, to say that my mother had been in a car accident, and was in a coma. I don't know if the whiskey made it better of worse, but I was frozen, shocked, unable to cry, scream or even move. It was then I realized the reason for the intense, sudden, emotional drop I experienced earlier during the show. Finally, still in a haze, I finished the whiskey and asked to call my sister, who gave me sketchy details of what had happened. I looked at the telephone receiver as if the words coming through this instrument could not possibly be true, and totally lost it, going into a screaming, crying frenzy. When I finally gathered myself, I shakily explained to my sister that I only had two more days of shows to do, but was coming home immediately. After some back and forth between us, and over my strenuous objections, my sister was adamant that I remain in Milan, insisting that there was nothing I could do at the hospital but wait like the rest of the family, so I should complete my shows, and that she would call me if there was any change. Those who really knew me knew that I adored my mother. Though she doubted I would have any success at modeling, she was so proud of my accomplishments, and stuck by me, despite my fathers' discontent with my career. Memories of her slowly began to surface. Being a fashion maven, she dressed impeccably, and was the one who instilled in me, my life-long love of fashion. How she would dress my sisters and I in matching outfits on Sundays, spend hours on end straightening our hair, and we were well dressed in school. Standing 5'10" herself, she was adamant about having good posture, constantly correcting my preteen stooping rounded shoulders, as I crossed my arms, always telling me to hold my head up, and be proud of my height, as well as my circumstances at all times.

Meanwhile, I was completely flummoxed. Stay and work while my mother is in a coma? How the hell was I to manage that? My stage presence, beauty, personality, and pizzazz all come from my happiness within! The words of the show-business anthem came to me; "the show must go on" regardless of what difficulties you as a performer are experiencing.

With the best of intentions, Tiziana called my two great friends, Billie Blair and Suzanne Czeh to stay with me for the evening. To their credit, and I bless them for it, they tried their best to sympathize and humor me, but nothing worked, I was beyond comforting, and just wanted to be alone to digest it all. Somehow, I got through the next two days of shows, and I actually was able to, (more or less), pull off my trademark excitement on the runway. After the last show, Tiziana made all the arrangements to get me on the first flight back to New York. Once back in my apartment in New York, I called the hospital in Portland, to find out my mother was still in a coma, and I was again told to just wait. Knowing how attached I was to my mother I think my sisters wanted to spare me the agony of seeing her in her present helpless condition. So I waited…and waited…through many phone calls to the hospital, and restless nights.

A few days later, I was at home, just exhausted from stress, and fell into a deep sleep on my sofa. I dreamt very vividly of my mother's spirit rising up to the heavens, so vividly that it startled me awake. I frantically reached for the telephone, and called the hospital. The nurse, who knew me as the "New York City daughter" by now, told me my mother had expired about five minutes ago. Once again, I was connected mysteriously, and powerfully to the spiritual world, which I am so grateful for. I thanked her, and I don't know how I was able to call my family, because my hands were shaking so, but I reached them, and told them Mom had passed—they hadn't heard yet, but was stunned when I told them how I had realized, and found out that our mother was gone. I hung up the phone, and while I was packing my bags, made arrangements to pick up my children.

The date is forever etched in my memory; April 12, 1981. We arrived in Portland, for the funeral, the following day. I was greeted by my mothers' brother, my Uncle Elmo, who gave me the biggest, longest and most memorable, comforting bear hug I've ever had. My father planned a small private family service, because he claimed he couldn't stand all the singing and crying, and carrying on that usually came with a Black funeral. The family all realized, however, it was because of his infidelity and mistreatment of my mother, and the guilt of seeing her friends. My mother's car collision happened in my father's vintage, limited edition, Buick, which was rammed into a wall, next door to my father's girlfriend's house. We will never know if it was suicide or an accident, nevertheless, as I laid my mother to rest, I knew in my heart, that nothing in my life would ever be the same again.

I stayed in Portland for a week, attending to family chores, sorting through paperwork, and assorted memorabilia, offering comfort as best I could while simultaneously receiving visits and condolences from friends. On April 17, my birthday, I was on a plane, coming home from my mothers' funeral, how ironic and sad. As I looked from the plane, at the snow-capped Mount

St. Helens, I realized just how life is; beautiful, precious, fast, and full of surprises. I decided then, to bring my children to New York to live with me.

After carefully researching the public and private neighborhood schools, I found a nice Catholic school for my children. With my busy schedule, I knew from experience I needed help, and had the great, good fortune of finding a marvelous nanny named Eutrice Roget, whom we called Brenda, to care for my young charges. I set about the task of moving my children from their home in Washington, D.C., to my apartment on Central Park West, (this time with no drama). Leon, who by this time realized I wasn't coming back to DC, had gone over and beyond the call of his duty as a father, put up no resistance. Rediscovering and exploring the great metropolis of New York City through the eyes of my children, turned out to be an extraordinarily enlightening and enjoyable experience for us all. They loved Central Park; we could walk everywhere, so many exciting stores and places for them to visit at any time... Between shuttling back and forth from the Catskill's bungalow, (which they thoroughly enjoyed), to our new apartment, the summer seemed to fly, and almost before I realized it, the time had come to enroll the children in school for the fall.

Coinciding with the school season, the September fashion season in Europe began, dictating that I return to work the runways once again. With my wonderful nanny Brenda in charge, I left for Europe encountering the most successful season financially and professionally, ever. I worked for all the top designers, one creation being more extravagant than the next, traveled to more exotic places, was being paid extremely well...but something was missing. Seeing the world, and all its many wonders, alone, was just no fun. I slowly came to understand that I needed something more in my life, namely, companionship, both the presence of my children and a romantic interest. I needed someone with whom I could share the pleasures and joys of my life. The line from the Mahogany movie says it best; "success is nothing without someone to share it with". I realized then, how lonely a modeling career could be. You have to be flexible, foot loose, (if not exactly fancy free), literally ready and willing to move from one side of the globe to the other, at any given moment, alone. I researched the aspects of buying an apartment or club in Paris, but there was so much red tape involved, even though I was paying cash, I decided against it. So when the season ended, determined to put an end to this loneliness, I decided to, (gulp!), retire.

CHAPTER TWENTY-TWO

Café Shailah

W ithout telling anyone in the industry about my plans or intentions, I gathered all my belongings in Paris, to make what I fully intended at the time, to be my final trip back home to New York City. As was my habit, I took the salary I had earned in cash, as usual hiding it on and "in" my body, and in my clothing before I departed. My rather unsophisticated upbringing somehow made me distrust anything but cash, and my natural caution inclined me to keep my money in places where I could account for it at all times. Having nearly $20,000 literally "on me" in cash, hidden in all the usual places, I boarded the plane to Kennedy airport, and upon arrival this time, I was more nervous than ever, perhaps because this was the largest haul I'd ever had on one flight, and the limit at that time was $12,000. In truth, I felt like a "mule" carrying contraband drugs across the border! I guess my skittishness and discomfort must have shown; clearly something about me must have tipped off the customs inspectors, because for the first time, my possessions were examined like never before. An agent opened my bag carefully, and methodically, examining all of the contents. I don't know if I was blushing—my face certainly felt hot—as he found thick wads of bills rolled up in socks, secreted in the pockets of my suitcase, spirited away in my toiletry bag, hidden in neatly folded piles of clothes, just seemingly everywhere, and I knew I was in a panic. I was asked to step out of the line, and was taken into a small room where I was questioned by a squadron of security personnel: Who was I?

Where was I coming from? Where did almost $20,000 in cash come from?...and on and on. Fortunately, as nervous as I was, I remembered that I also had receipts, vouchers, and other proof that the money represented my legitimate earnings, that I was not an international jewel thief or some other such unsavory miscreant, and that I had done nothing illegal. (Keep good records!) Finally, one of the officers told me that the matter would have to be investigated. In the meantime, they would confiscate all but two thousand dollars of my stash, until the following day when they would have had time to verify my story. I was relieved the ordeal was over, but devastated as I collected my belongings. As hard as I had worked for that money, I knew in my heart I was getting my money back, as the immortal words of Malcolm X quotes, "by any means necessary".

Not surprisingly, I found myself unable to sleep well that night, and, early the next morning, I called the customs office, explained who I was, and asked to speak to someone in charge of investigations. Miraculously, I was told that all was clear, and was given directions to the customs office to retrieve my money. Clearly, I still had many more lessons to learn in the course of my life, but this one was impressed upon me with crystalline clarity; never, (for a variety of safety and security reasons), carry large amounts of cash with you when traveling. Either arrange for a wire transfer or take advantage of the more sophisticated ways to deposit money electronically, so that it can be withdrawn as needed. I doubt if my money would be so easily returned these days.

OK, now that I was "retired", what was I to do next. I had been discussing very lightly with my new neighbors, Jean Francois and Clarence Gamblin, both masters of cuisine, who owned a cute little café at 333 West 86th street between West End

Avenue and Riverside Drive, about purchasing their business. They had been in the business for years, and had grown tired of it. Although I couldn't cook worth a shit, which should have been sufficient to put the kibosh on any quixotic plans I had to embark on such an unlikely course of action, impetuosity was one of my virtues, to be free, open, to go with the flow. I thought it would be a great family business experience for my children, and it would serve as the perfect way for me to transition out of the fashion business, and into another line of work, with a ready-made establishment and clientele. Without another moment's hesitation, I bought the cafe.

With my customary gusto, I frantically went through all the classes to obtain the health certificate, permits, obtaining referrals to purveyors and suppliers, and, unbelievably, within a few weeks I was able to celebrate the grand opening of Shailah's Café. My chef was fantastic, and my eldest son Anthony totally enjoyed doing the endless tasks that were required to keep the place humming, while developing great cooking skills as well.

I learned fast that this was no easy business. As anyone who has ever tried to run a restaurant knows only too well, running an eatery literally demands every moment of your time. I arrived daily at 6:30 A.M. to meet my suppliers, and assist my chef to prep for the day. We were open for breakfast, lunch and dinner, six days a week. A schedule no sane person would even think of undertaking alone, let alone a neophyte in the restaurant business. I usually didn't leave until eight or nine P.M. every evening, which caused my social life to take a nosedive, but I was committed, thoroughly enjoyed the feeling of being in charge, and the opportunity and responsibility I was giving my children. We had great times and well into the year,

I had the idea to add a piano, and hire performers, to enhance the ambiance. The entertainment never happened.

Once again, the direction of my life was about to take a drastic and totally unexpected turn, leading me, almost in spite of myself, back to where I truly and rightfully belonged. I was mingling with my guests one day in the café, when I saw someone I recognized. It was Luis Costa, the assistant to Lisandro Sarasola, a brilliant designer of suede and leather fashions from Argentina, for whom I had modeled for, several times in New York. I had actually been somewhat of his muse, doing fittings, photo shoots and shows. Luis and I had become great friends, and after a warm greeting, he looked at me with astonishment and disbelief that I was totally not a model anymore. In his adorable Latino accent, he hastily said in one breath "Shailah, I heard you were here, are you out of your mind? Are you sure this is what you want to do?" he asked. Although it wasn't heaven, I was totally comfortable with my new vocation, and bravely answered, "This is my life now, Luis, I'm in it, and I can't turn back now." Being one of my biggest admirers as a model, he replied. "Oh, yes you can!" he said, "Lisandro is looking for a model for a major ad he's taking out in Vogue magazine. You know he always loved working with you. If you'd like I can suggest you." Everyone in the industry by this time knew I had children and my real age, so I'd given up the thought of ever being in Vogue, or recognized by the upper echelon of fashion runway or print. However, an old familiar thrill of excitement went through me at the thought of it, but I hoped I looked nonchalant, when I breezily said, "Okay, sure, if you want."

The very next day, Luis called to say Lisandro had agreed, and wanted to see me as soon as possible for details. Within a day, I hired someone to work in the café the rest of the week, and made plans to meet Lisandro. It was as if we had never stopped working together; both of us felt so comfortable with each other again. He wanted me to pose for the very important fall fashion September issue of Vogue magazine! (You gotta have friends..) I glowed as he gave me details for the shoot. At some point you have to realize, you cannot avoid your fate. The following week I was shooting a Vogue ad, which went extremely well, and I was waiting with baited breath for the publication in September. Soon after, Lisandro asked me to be the fit model, and muse for a new Italian line he was designing for, called Alma. The words were music to my ears—muse and fit model! Not only that, he asked me to go to Milan, Italy with him, to present the collection to the elite Italian clientele. How could I refuse? We did the most fabulous photo to advertise the presentation in Milan, and Lisandro had it blown up to life size. It has remained one of my favorites, and that very photograph, in fact, of me posing like an Erte statue in an amazing black satin rhinestone trimmed dress, is what I selected for the cover of this book!

It felt great to be back in Milan, the show was fabulous, with an unforgettable finale. For the finale I had to walk into the life size picture of myself, and stand in the exact pose. I was the photo come to life, a perfect tableaux vivant, and the audience went wild! Fabulous!

Though my stay was short, I saw many familiar faces at the show, including designers who remembered me, and asking why they had not seen me recently, and encouraged me to resume my modeling career. It felt right and moreover, I realized now that I missed the modeling life, as hectic, lonely, and maddening as it was, and that it was probably the passing and mourning of my mother that had caused my sentimentality, and rash lifestyle change into the café business. I was ready to make my comeback, but there was a fly in the ointment. What was I to do with the restaurant? Well you know the scenario by now, my best friend "fate", stepped in again, and provided circumstances that would resolve the situation for me once again.

When I returned to New York, I immediately went to check on the café. Anyone who knows anything about cooking on a grill knows that it has to be thoroughly scrubbed clean at least once or twice a day. The lazy person I had hired to be in charge, obviously had not cleaned it once, and it was burned completely black. The cashier I hired claimed, there was no profit for the week. Of course not!!! A stranger handling my cash business, what was I thinking? Needless to say, they both were thrown out immediately.

I had a message awaiting me from the café's building manager, Simon, to see him immediately. I assumed the urgency was about my absence, or renewing my lease, but instead, I was told that renovations had to be made to the café to meet the new required building codes. The total cost would be in the neighborhood of $25,000, a pretty pricey neighborhood for me, and I had to consider my options. Was it worth the investment? Was I really happy here? I'd had some very profitable days in the restaurant business financially, but was pretty much breaking even most of the time. I decided to immediately begin to search for an appraiser to analyze the situation.

The appraiser arrived the following day, and after looking over my books, the location of the cafe, and assessing other business aspects, he told me to sell the place, as he couldn't see business getting any better in that location. It was off the beaten track of a major thoroughfare, and the business from neighborhood locals, though loyal, was just not enough to provide a profitable future. After buttonholing as many business people as I could, and making endless telephone calls, within two weeks, I sold everything in the café that wasn't tied down. As luck would have it, I also found a buyer for the restaurant, who agreed to pay me exactly what I paid for it a year before. I was so grateful that I didn't lose my shirt on this one. God is Great.

That problem solved, I was free from a brave and daring business venture that proved wrong for me. With no regrets, and great anticipation, I looked forward to picking up where I left off, and getting back to the runway where I belonged. I had traveled a long, circuitous road to find myself once again guided by the hand of fate, back to the beginning, back to the fashion world that I knew and loved. Look out, modeling world, "Shailah" was back in town. The beauty was back on duty!

Bernard Perris - Paris for Harpers Bazaar Magazine 1988

NEW YORK PRINT

RUDY LEPENSKI

EBONY MAGAZINE-BILL BLASS
(Photo:Moneta Sleet Jr.)

SEPTEMBER VOGUE

LISANDRO SARASOLA
(Photos: David Zahner)

NATIONAL CIGARETTE ADS

INTERVIEW MAGAZINE-ERIC BEAMON JEWELRY (Photo: George DuBose)

WOMANS WEAR DAILY COVERS

W MAGAZINE

Karl Lagerfeld for Fendi, with his bevy of models

Bastille Day Party at Maxim's

186

NEW YORK TIMES

Dior Mink NY Skyline coat Versace with Billie Blair Pauline Trigere's fitting model
(NY Times photos: Bill Cunningham)

Stephen Burrows   Valerie Louthan   Gianfranco Ferre   Pat Iuto Fur

Mary Jane Denzer

Sassoon Jean Ad

Keith Haring Gala Dinner
With Fred Schneider of The B52's

Metropolitan Museum of Art
Costume Gala

Leaving a Met Gala
with chauffeur

Presenting a caftan I modeled
to film legend Jane Russell

NEW YORK SHOWS

CHAPTER TWENTY-THREE

The Runway to Success

I managed to pick up where I left off in the modeling business, my agents taking me back with open arms, and I found myself quickly back on the runway circuit. My life and career as a high-fashion model continued—as is the case for all performers with longevity who realizes they are in a business—with some very great highs, interspersed with various lows, over the next six or seven years. With the love of music still coursing through my veins, in my spare time, I was singing backup with local groups, even a rock band! One of my great highs, was when I did my first professional backup singing job, with Fred Schneider, (of B'52s fame). I was cast for a show with an amazing New York designer, Robert Molnar, who loved my sense of wildness and humor, as much as I did his designs. I would go out regularly to dinners and dancing with a group of his friends, which entailed lots of belly aching laughs, dancing and great times. Little did I know that one of the members of our group was Fred! We called ourselves the Wing Dings, and on occasion would dress in wild costumes, made of the cheapest polyester, purchased from Fred's favorite thrift stores, and hit the hot clubs in the city. Well, by that time we were like family and Fred knew the real me, whom he liked so well that he invited me to sing backup with him on his solo album, not to mention we even considered marriage! I am pictured on his album cover "The Shake Society" holding the boom box. I'd heard the B52's hit, Rock Lobster, in college, but it certainly wasn't on my top ten list, and I had no idea how much clout the B52's had. I finally realized it, when I was invited to be their featured dancer, go-go style on top of a tall glass column, to a capacity audience at the renowned Radio City Music Hall. Lesson here: Always be yourself.

* * *

I'd managed to give my children a decent life and maintain a respectable reputation and career; however, throughout the years, especially in Europe, I continued to shelter the fact from models and clients, that I had children, not only because it made a model seem old, but it would reveal my true age, which I still deducted 10-15 years from, when asked. This was a time I couldn't be myself because of the nuances of the business, and personally I found it boring to talk about children with all the glamour, and fabulous excitement that went on backstage. I've always been somewhat of a private person anyway, but when the few professional people I let into my personal life asked about them, I would claim them as cousins or nephews, and I was never questioned, though by this time, they probably knew I was lying.

Due to my busy schedule, I was again too busy to spend a lot of time with my children, resulting in a lot of unsupervised time for both of them, which was really dangerous, now that they were in their pre-teen and teenage years. My oldest succumbed to the result of not having an attentive parent, and had some tumultuous occurrences. I soon realized he was becoming attached to the wrong friends and circumstances, which prompted me to again, send him back to Washington, DC to live with his father. New York was just too dangerous, and he was an intelligent, bored kid, a very perilous combination. Not comfortable with being alone, my other son expressed the desire to go to military boarding school. There he would have the camaraderie of a roommate, and companionship, not to mention unlimited food, (he loved to eat!). I began researching military schools, and found a nice, affordable one, called Fork Union Military Academy, tucked away deep in a small town, in Fork Union, Virginia. A quiet, friendly town, similar to Mayberry on the Andy Griffith shows. It was totally safe, not directly associated with the military, and he fit in perfectly, so I immediately paid cash for his four years there. (My cash flow was flourishing!) So here I was, alone again, traveling the world, doing what I was born to do, yet making the ultimate sacrifice. Sometimes, life just isn't fair, but you must embrace it, and play with the cards that are dealt to you, with a smile.

One thing I'd noticed over the years was that black models did not work as much during the winter collections, as they did for the summer collections. The "excuse" was that the bland colors of fall didn't show up as well on dark skin, as the bright colors of spring and summer did. As I said, an "excuse" and a senseless one as well, but one even I had to accept, each year not expecting a financially lucrative season during the fall/winter season of shows.

In Europe, you never feel the blatant sense of racism like you do in America. There, you were known as an American model, period. Though rejected sometimes because I was black, I never focused on, or sulked about "being" black. I respected the fact that the shows had to maintain a variety of ethnicities, and I was treated with the utmost respect wherever I went. I was a good, professional model, and that was it.

The top runway models during my era were Iman, Pat Cleveland and Billie Blair. Though I was now somewhat on their level, had befriended them all, and we had the highest respect for each other, we didn't socialize together after the shows. As a matter of fact, I had no real model friends, but being somewhat of a loner, I didn't mind. Let's be real, we were all out for the same thing, and competition was fierce amongst us. The top one, Iman was cordial, but acted like royalty, and always had her own entourage. She didn't readily accept models into her circle that wasn't on her level of popularity. Pat Cleveland always had men around her, gay or straight, she was always being pampered by someone, or putting on her show for someone, but Billie Blair was somewhat of a loner, down to earth, and more approachable. I had long admired her svelte figure and gazelle like movements on the runway. She was a huge inspiration to me and early on, I was determined to befriend her in hopes that some of her magic would rub off on me☺ I later learned that I had my own magic.

During the fashion season in Milan, after one of the final shows of the day, I asked to hang out with her. When I asked what she liked to do, she replied, "Just a nice dinner, and you know what else I like." I had no idea but I said, "Maybe smoke a joint, and go to the club?" which was my usual. "Oh nooo", she said, I like the white powder". After realizing she wasn't' talking about makeup powder, I told her I didn't do cocaine, and knew very little about it, but we went to dinner, and a club, and had a fun night anyway. She wasn't much of a dancer or club-loving person as I was, and was anxious to get back to her room. So I cut my night short, and went back to her room. After hanging out there for a while, and watch her feverishly inhaling that white powder, I realized she had a cocaine addiction.

Everyone has their demon, and I lost no respect for her, it just wasn't my thing. Though I detected a slight competition, and jealousy undertone from her, (which was normal between models) we remained very good friends, but I knew it could only go so far with this substance in the picture. A few years later, that demonic substance ultimately destroyed her life, and career, but she has now healed, is doing well, and we have remained friends to this day.

The more I hung out in Milan, however, the more I realized that cocaine was rampant within the fashion industry, and sure enough, I began to try a bit here and there. The Italian playboys would be waiting for us after the shows, with a supply of the top quality dust. They treated us like royalty, dinners, clubs, shopping...It was fun, and I loved the high, but it seemed I always got sick the next day or two after I did it, so I listened to my body, and avoided overdoing it, mostly faking it when it was passed to me more than twice. (Just say NO!) It seemed the models that did the most, worked the most, but I never felt I needed to compete that way, and was still fine toking on a joint once in a while. Pot made me laugh and sing and have fun. I guess subconsciously my children kept me grounded in that way as well. By now some of the European models agents knew about my children, but everyone was very respectful, never questioning me about it, and I later found out I wasn't the only model who had lied about their age and children. My agents kept the hush about me, because by this time, I was making big money for them, and my friends knew as an Aries, I was not one to be reckoned with if I ever found out they had blabbed. So between being somewhat straight-laced, and having children, I never made it as a superstar model, but I was damn good, made good money, and held my own against any of the best competition.

I maintained my Central Park West apartment with ease, managed to visit my children often, took a few trips to my hometown of Portland, while jet-setting to and from Europe, and life was somewhat of a breeze, until I found out about the new hot club, Studio 54.

CHAPTER TWENTY-FOUR

Let's Dance!

B eing a top model, one is somewhat of a celebrity, and Internationally, you had to be seen in all of the hot spots. You absolutely could not go to Paris or Milan and say you'd never been to Studio 54, Xenon, Area, Limelight, or the hottest disco. God forbid! I don't think there are words to explain how incredibly fabulous Studio 54 club was, packed with celebrities, great music, top designers, fashion, gorgeous models, DRUGS and debauchery everywhere. With my love of music, and great dancing skills, once I got started, I would dance easily for an hour non-stop. My dancing inspired other people, and I always had a circle or crowd around me, watching or joining in. One of my treasured pictures in Womens Wear Daily, is of me dancing with Marc Bohan, who was then the designer of Christian Dior. Genuine European royalty and the royalty of show business flocked to these venues. I danced with the likes of Sylvester Stallone, Jack Nicholson, Monsieur Givenchy, to name a few I can remember. I was such a regular patron at 54, that the management threw ME a birthday party, at this hot spot! It's all somewhat of a blur now, because most nights would not end until 6AM, and I would just come home, shower, change clothes, and go straight to work a show, or showroom. I did my share of drugs there as well, got plenty ripped, and had big fun, but again, never to the point of abuse. One of my mother's favorite quotes was "Ya gotta know when the party is over", and I always held close to that. Yet, needless to say, I did get somewhat ensnared into the drug scene a bit, had my share of casual trysts, but again for the fun and enjoyment of it. (Wow, what cocaine did for sex was incredible!)

Eventually I began to lose the enjoyment for cocaine, not only because of the constant respiratory ailments, but I had hit the bottom of the barrel as far as friends and acquaintances went. They would call or come to my apartment in the wee hours of the morning looking for someone to share the drug with. I felt myself spiraling downward, and I knew I had to stop; it was just a matter of when and how.

One of my fellow model friends, Arlethia Horton, who was very popular in Milan, had gotten hooked on cocaine. She was one of the friends who would call me at 3 or 4 in the morning, complaining about work being slow and other chatter. She was currently living with her dealer, who kept her in a constant haze, and her career had taken a major downward spiral because of this. One night, towards the end of her life, she was very high, and called me from a phone booth at the usual wee hour, telling me she had no electricity because she couldn't pay her bill, and the men she was dealing with, especially the one that lived with her, were after her for money. I comforted her as best I could without being too involved. Two days later I received a call from a friend, to tell me that she was either pushed, or jumped from her balcony, and was dead. I was devastated, and took it as a sure wake up call. This was truly a sign of where my life was going if I continued this drug, so I searched my apartment for every type of drug or paraphernalia I had, throwing them out the window and flushing them down the toilet. I must've cried for three hours straight, and gradually dropped every friend that was associated with that drug.

There was so much debauchery that entangled my career, and life, during the legendary Studio 54 era. I had another physical altercation with a model I found cheating with my boyfriend, as well as wielded a knife on him. On one occasion, I had a test photo shoot with a photographer recommended by a friend. While preparing for the shoot, I couldn't take my eyes off of the gorgeous man on the other side of the room that seemed to be rolling a joint. After the shoot, I was introduced to him as Calvin Lockhart, the star actor of so many major black films! Before I knew it, we were smoking together, and within a week, we were dating. Due to lies, demands and drugs, our relationship didn't last long, just another blur of ecstasy and good times, but gawd he was gorgeous!

During that time, the boyfriends came and went. Some great, but most not so great. Most of them just wanted sex. Many men were intimidated by my success, and just wanted to party, with no commitment, and others couldn't deal with my motherhood. Realizing I was getting nowhere in the love department, I decided to clean my slate in that area as well, and dedicate myself totally to my career.

Whether you have children or not, any part of show business or being a celebrity is very lonely. Hard work and discipline is MAJOR in the business, and due to long hours and travel, you rarely have time for negative, unproductive distractions. You are constantly on the move, answering to the beckoning calls from your agent, flying from state to state or sometimes country to country within a week, taking instructions from photographers, designers etc. It's hectic to say the least, so enduring a successful relationship is difficult, and often times you'd rather be alone, than with someone who stresses about your availability. Sometimes you just want to say "F" it and go on a fun binge, but you have to have a strong will, and a love of self and your career. If you love your career, it is your drug and your lover.

Family support is very important in show business. If you don't have it, make sure you have a circle or just one supportive "real" friend to turn to when in need of moral support. The models I knew that lost it along the way had neither, and I truly owe my sister Marian my life, because she was always there for me to vent to, and was always at the ready, with sound advice to help in time of need.

One of my favorite pastimes is writing poetry, (a book to come soon) which I did a lot of, during my travels and adventures. During this renewal time that I was going through, I began to write again, as a way to vent my feelings of some of the loneliness and despair that I experienced along the way. One must find ways to keep your mind happy, such as exercise, classes, volunteering, etc. Especially now with the Internet, the world is at your fingertips to try new hobbies and adventures. After witnessing friends and models experience mental breakdowns, drug addictions, and death, I can't stress this enough. Performing arts take a toll on you emotionally, and everything is exaggerated and distorted when drugs are involved...Don't do drugs!!!

After a few more years, my career in Europe began to fade, as the business goes, the newer breed and style of model replaced me. Models that never smiled on the runway, never turned, lifted their arms or expressed flair of any type. It was all about the Supermodel, models who had the name, Linda Evangelista, Christie Turlington, Naomi Campbell, Claudia Schiffer, Tyra Banks...but could not necessarily walk with any showmanship. They were overexposed on every major magazine cover, extensive fashion spreads, fashion or TV ads, so when they appeared on the runway, the crowds went wild, screaming their names, and bought everything they wore. Iman was the only one from my era who managed to cross over into that market comfortably, but didn't stay there long.

When I was told initially that I wasn't booked for my favorite European designers shows, it was devastating and heartbreaking. As a model, one must realize when your heyday in one market is over, it's time to move on to the next market that is comfortable for you. My last hurrah was in Rome for a spectacular couture show using a retrospect of top Italian models of the 80's. It was grand, at night with 100 black stallions prancing in formation, and Natalie Cole singing, as show openers. When I was told she was singing, I grabbed Pat Cleveland and busted into her dressing room to meet her. She was so gracious and granted me a photo with her. I strutted that over 200 foot plexiglas, under lit runway like the resplendent stallion I was, and rode off with a gorgeous Carabinieri, (who was riding one of the horses), on a moto after the show. What a way to end an incredible couture career!

My next market was showroom modeling where, although it was a harder job, I managed to make a very good living at it for many years. Showroom modeling is where a model or group of models, show the designers collection privately to the store buyers, or press, after the major show season. The hours were long, sometimes 8-10 hours a day and you could try on well over two hundred garments a day for the constant flow of department store buyers. It's very fast paced, the more garments you show, the more the designer sold, and I'd developed a reputation as one of the fastest changers, so I worked a lot. Sometimes my earlobes would be sore at the end of the season from pulling clothing over my head so often. Imagine! It was still seasonal work, lasting 2-3 weeks after the major fashion season, and the money wasn't what I'd been used to, but I adjusted easily. I must interject here, the importance of being nice and personable to your booker. My showroom period was during the time when the AIDS epidemic was taking lives at a rapid pace. I was currently with Faces Agency, being booked by Gary White. His assistant, James who had become a great friend, told me on his dying bed, how Gary would blatantly tell my showroom clients that I was not available, so he could book his favorite model of the moment. I was so hurt, and pissed off because I was still supporting my children. He knew the go-getter that I was, would find someone else to hire me. Gary had passed away before James; otherwise I would've had some choice words for him! So take your booker flowers, and chocolates, etc, be personable; show you are grateful for their hard work.

When showroom season ended, it left time for me to pursue both commercial and fashion print work, singing, and taking classes to prepare myself for the next phase of my life. In any part of show business, realize you will NEVER stay on top forever. It's ALWAYS wise to have a plan B, to cushion your fall from stardom.

PARTY PIX

Hamming it up with the stars of the film, The Lost Boys, the late Corey Haim and Corey Feldman. Models (l-r) Soos Packard, Marianna Verkerk (notice her earrings!) LucyAnn Barry, Eugenie

The Wing Dings, created by Fred Schneider with Robert Molnar and gang

Studio 54 Birthday Invite

With Calvin Lockhart, film star in an After Hours joint

Shailah Edmonds and Marc Bohan

It was a different crowd that turned out later that evening at Xenon for a party in Marc Bohan's honor (photos bottom left). The designer chatted with Odile Rubirosa before taking to the dance floor with one of his models, Shailah Edmonds. Pele, the soccer star, also showed off his fancy footwork with Teresa Sodre. Xenon regular Jamie Blandford, son of the Duke of Marlborough, also danced with Louise Steele, while Prince Christian de Massy (son of Prince Rainier's sister, Antoinette) with Countess Michelle Sutkan, the Count Olivier de Chandon, of the champagne family, with Claudia Vallanzuela, watched from the sidelines.
— PAULA MAGDALENA

Featured in Womens Wear Daily, Dancing at Xenon with Marc Bohan

CHAPTER TWENTY-FIVE

Using My Expertise

O ne July, I was booked for a fashion show for an organization that held modeling competitions, called the IMTA. As I looked out into the audience at the hundreds of aspiring models, it brought back such memories of how I started in my small competition years ago. Then a light bulb went off! I was so inspired that I wanted to speak to these models, and tell them that it was possible to make it into the mainstream, from being in a model competition. (Well, it's a start anyway). After the show, I went to the front desk of the hotel, and asked who the President of the organization was. I was given the name Helen Rogers, and immediately went to the phone to call her. She promptly answered the phone, and I gave her my schpiel, which she readily accepted, and invited me to her room right away. Without missing a beat, I headed for the elevators. A very chic lady answered the door giving me a warm welcome, however I could tell she was a shrewd businesswoman. After giving her the short version of my background, she asked me to stand up, and give her a sample of my speech right then and there, of what I would say to aspiring models. I must say my heart skipped a beat, but she never knew it, because the words flowed out of my mouth like the river Nile. That's chutzpah and confidence unbridled! She hired me on the spot, and I began doing seminars for her organization, which continued for over 15 years, and paid handsomely.

I truly loved sharing my experience with these aspiring models that were hungry, and so appreciative for the information coming from an industry professional. Modeling school directors from this organization would hire me privately, flying me out to all parts of the USA, to teach my seminars in their schools, for a lofty fee. I was in such demand that I couldn't handle them all. One director was so disappointed that I couldn't fit her into my schedule that she suggested I do a video with all my information, and sell it! Brilliant idea! I followed up on the idea immediately, producing a well-received video entitled "How To Become A Successful Runway Model", (I even sang the theme song!), which sold well to every modeling school and most agencies nationwide. As with any art, you grow and get better with practice and experience, and there are changes in the industry, so after a few years, I produced a second video/DVD, entitled The Runway To Success, which was longer, more informative, and sold ten times better than the first one, for many years, again to every modeling school, agency, and aspiring model in the business. Through my website, runwaytotsuccess.com, (now, shailahedmonds.com), it even shipped Internationally, and David Vando of Models Mart, a model supply store, (the angel that he is), sold it retail as well. It was the first modeling video to be put into the library for the hearing impaired. I wish I could remember the director who suggested that I do the video so I could thank her, because it led me into a completely new career.

Just when the showroom modeling began to phase out for me, I had established myself in the commercial print market, and had a lucrative coaching business with schools and agencies Nationwide. For those of you who fail to plan ahead like I did, listen to your inner voice, meditate, PRAY, have a strong spiritual connection, and any idea that comes to you, have the courage to try it. I am living proof that it works!

There is no union, or any place to go for retired models, and failure to plan was the downfall of most models that experienced a downward spiral emotionally and financially when their career ended. One must learn to stay a step ahead of your game.

HOW TO BE
A SUCCESSFUL
RUNWAY MODEL

by International Model
Shailah Edmonds

CHAPTER TWENTY-SIX

Know The "Business"

O verall, I have to say that I have been very blessed, and am proud and grateful for my modeling career and the International success I've achieved; Flying the now defunct Concorde supersonic jet, which took me from New York City to London in three hours, going to Denzel Washington's house, getting a tour by the master actor himself, being photographed by Andy Warhol, the amazing celebrity parties, backstage passes to any concert, are just a hint of the many highlights of my career.

I must address however, today, these things are not as easy to accomplish, simply because competition is fiercer than ever, and demand is down because there are fewer designers and models now are competing with celebrities as well. There are so many misconceptions, misunderstandings, and misperceptions about the modeling business, be it haute couture or in any other area, of modeling. You realize from this book, all the chances you have to take, the drive, the thick skin… So many harsh realities must be understood and accepted, if you wish to have any hope of being a successful fashion model.

The unfortunate emergence of so-called reality shows on television, which purport to be about being able to catapult a young girl to the front lines of the fashion industry, does a disservice both to the young participants involved who have dreams of becoming a top model, as well as to those watching who receive an unrealistic picture of what the industry is really all about. The blunt truth is that winning, or not winning, a reality

TV modeling show competition, is no guarantee of having a real career in the fashion industry. Worse, some girls might get the impression that not being the winner of one of these shows means that the national exposure that comes with losing, means that they have little or no hope of becoming a fashion model. It's heartbreaking to think of how many egos are shattered, and self-esteem compromised, by an overemphasis on these kinds of reality shows. There is no doubt that you do not ever have to appear on a television reality show if you wish to enter the modeling world, and if you do appear, that it is most definitely not an automatic express lane to fame and fortune.

It is also true that, as with many other areas of the performing arts, the field is oriented toward youth; successful models start out at a very young age, more so now than ever. It takes discipline, hard work, practice, patience, self-confidence, and training to develop your skills, therefore models should start working on building a budding career while they're still in their teens; thirteen to sixteen, is not too young to begin learning the ropes, and is the age agents are looking for today. As incredible as it may seem, after the age of twenty-two, you will be considered too old to begin a career as a runway model, however you can pursue commercial print modeling.

Learn the requirements of being a fashion model from the ground up. FIRST AND FOREMOST, be aware of the height and size requirements. (5'10-11and size 2 (32-34-34). If you don't meet them, don't waste your time. Follow the fashion trends. Learn about fabrics, how to move like a model, the rudiments of working the runway, learning how to relate to the camera, and what it takes to "come alive" when that camera clicks, and how to properly nourish and care for your growing body.

Some girls begin getting accustomed to developing the poise to walk confidently on stage by entering pageants; still others get their first public exposure by working on theatrical productions in school or doing local fashion shows. However you choose to start, get comfortable with the stage and camera, you can't be shy in this business!

Just as important is the business of modeling. You cannot sit around waiting for the phone to ring to be discovered. You have to be an aggressive go-getter. Know that your career as a successful model means constantly reinventing yourself, learning new things, and adjusting to the changing demands of the industry. Always look for a way to market yourself, and network, showing the utmost enthusiasm for the business. SOCIAL MEDIA IS HUGE AND VITALLY IMPORTANT TO HAVE.

Whether, like me, you come from a humble background, or had the good fortune to be born with a silver spoon in your mouth, you should know that modeling is a craft to be learned. You must develop your technique and build a firm foundation, then develop your own personal style and flair. Models today are instructed to walk with very little movement and no personality, and I find it totally boring. However, it is still possible to maintain an aura of elegance and style with your eyes and attitude.

A potential model must be brutally honest about their needs and expectations. If it's predictability, a steady pay-check and a regularly scheduled routine that you need, I'm afraid modeling is not for you. Your entire life and career as a model are characterized by unpredictability, uncertainty, sporadic employment, and spontaneity. You must have a "go-with-the-flow" attitude. You literally never know from one day to the next when the telephone rings, what jobs may come your way or what might happen, and sometimes for no rational reason, in a matter of the shutter of the camera lens, one season you're hot, and the next you're not. Make no mistake, it is a highly competitive and tough business, and you need to be prepared for the obstacles that you will inevitably have to face. There is simply no substitute for having a level head and staying focused, aware always of keeping your eyes on the prize. I don't mean to sound preachy, but models that resort to abusing drugs or alcohol to cushion the blows, or to serve as a buffer for the ups and downs of their professional life, don't last very long.

Please remember always; it's not just about making a splash in the modeling world for a brief period. The key to successful modeling is longevity, being able to sustain a career by thinking ahead and being professional. Know your craft; be like a chameleon, changing your look and pictures to suit new times and circumstances. A successful model can expect to remain at the top of her game for about five years, but can remain in the business fifteen or twenty years. The fact that I have remained in the business for the better part of thirty years, which includes being a modeling coach, for ten of those years, is a testament to my awareness of the demands of the marketplace during each phase of my career.

If after a solid year of trying in every way that you can to become a model, and you still have not secured an agent or a modeling job, perhaps the field is not for you. But, before you give up, please get training or advice from a professional in the business, because you just may need some minor adjustments to your look, your walk or your attitude to succeed.

If you decide to recede from the modeling world, consider other careers or ancillary occupations, where you can still be associated with the fashion world. Perhaps a career as a makeup artist, hair stylist, fashion show producer, fashion designer, stylist, or working at a modeling agency as a booker, are a few options. Dressers for models are always in demand for the shows, and this is a great way to get hands on experience in the production end of the business. Furthering your education is always a good fallback position; apply to one of the specialized trade schools—the Fashion Institute of Technology, or Parsons School of Design in New York City are only two of many possibilities. I'm sure there are some schools in or near your city that offer a fashion-affiliated career, perhaps in business, design, or merchandising.

Another reality check to consider; some people have an idea that they only want to aspire to be a top model, sauntering down the runway for the world's most famous couturiers, that these models are the only "true" or "real" models. The reality is that just as most singers, even very fine singers, are not cut out to be opera singers, most aspiring models cannot realistically expect to walk the ultra-high fashion runways in Europe, Asia, and the world. Only a relatively very small, select group of models ever get to know the excitement of being a part of the haute couture market. You have to have that special "something" or a very good connection in the industry. I was very lucky, blessed, fortunate, and focused, which enabled me to be a part of that rarefied world. Just because you don't become a top or couture model, doesn't mean there's no place for you in the industry. In fact, most modeling jobs are not at all connected to the world of the haute couture.

There are many different facets, and niches within the modeling profession. If by temperament, physical attributes, or attitude you're just not cut out for top model status, be aware that you can have a rewarding and satisfying career as a showroom, bridal, swimwear, commercial print, catalogue, parts (models who only show their hands or feet etc.), or fit model, just to name a few of the specialized areas that accept shorter models. Moreover, don't expect or think that you have to rise to the level of having a "one-word" name—a Naomi, or a Christy or an Iman, to be a successful model. By dint of incredibly hard work, some luck, confidence, and a positive attitude, I've had a successful and lucrative International haute couture, and all other genres of a modeling career, for more than two decades, without ever becoming a household name!

Not to dwell on the pitfalls or overemphasize the "thorns" among the "roses" that you may encounter as an aspiring model, my purpose in talking about the real-life challenges that you must be prepared for is twofold: I want to paint as realistic a picture as possible about what any new model will be up against trying to break into and get consistent work in the industry; and, perhaps more important, I want anyone who has serious modeling aspirations to be aware of the daunting personal and professional responsibilities that he or she is undertaking, without any illusions, and without any of the misconceptions that so many people have, about what it means to be part of the industry.

As for the roses—ah, yes, the roses! Establishing yourself as a working model is an amazing accomplishment, and a life changing experience. With success comes the awareness that you have ascended to a very special realm, one, which most people in the whole world can never achieve. Also, no matter what other occupations exist for people to pursue, there is no feeling on earth that can compare with the excitement and exhilaration that comes with strutting down the runway, clothed in the most exquisitely made garments that, {a great deal of}, money can buy, fashioned from the rarest and most beautiful materials known to man, shaped by a master couturier who has created a wearable work of art. With each step down that runway, swathed in magnificent fabrics, your hair and makeup the epitome of groomed perfection, the audience applauding and sometimes shouting your name, not to mention the fringe benefits; along with the aforementioned, a model also receives endless clothing from designers who want them to be seen in their garments...—well, suffice it to say that there are few experiences in life that can compare!

CHAPTER TWENTY-SEVEN

The Digital Pros and Cons

No area of human activity has been exempt from the sweeping changes that the Internet has wrought, and the modeling world is no exception.

Gone are the days when you call to make an appointment to be seen in person by an agent. Everything is submitted online before any appointment is made. The downside of this is sometimes a picture can't capture your best assets, and you never get a chance to show your true self. To get the scoop on the modeling business today, I called upon Louise Roberts, former director of APM Models, (owned by Penny Basch), in New York City, a woman with more than forty years of experience in the modeling business, to fill me in on the latest information, and discuss in detail how the digital age has affected the industry.

When a client wants to see a model's portfolio of pictures, a messenger usually sends the portfolio to the client. "The use of messengers to send books to clients still happens, but much less than in the past". The client now asks for a video of the models walk, and pictures are sent digitally. If they are approved, the model gets called for a casting. With this system however, fewer clients need to see and touch the actual photographs, and models are sent on fewer actual go-sees and castings than ever. Most models have their portfolio on an Ipad, (be prepared for that investment). "However", Louise continued, "since most clients book online, agents are constantly sending in their model submissions online, a development Louise feels is not as beneficial, because the potential client is deprived of the passion and enthusiasm in the agents' vocal presentation when trying to sell a model, which makes it more difficult to entice a client to try a new girl. When you have talent, verbal communication is essential to conveying that talent to a client." (So make that personal casting work when you get it. Give lots of personality, and don't stop walking until you are asked to!)

One of the things that made Louise such an extraordinary and successful operator was her willingness, indeed, her determination, to defy the Internet policy, by calling her clients to speak to them directly, or at least to leave telephone messages in order to make the connection more personal.

"The upside of the Internet is, that it is absolutely possible for aspiring models these days to find an agent online. Agents receive and accept digital submissions worldwide all the time, and will respond if they are interested."

"E-mail and text messaging are most commonly used today to communicate with a model, which means that PDA's (personal digital assistant) are constantly beeping, or vibrating, something that can be very annoying in an office setting, but something that has to be accepted nevertheless." Again, Louise made a practice of calling her models regularly to ensure that they understand all the details of their bookings and castings.

"One other annoyance which must be endured", Louise went on, "is that sometimes you must text a model four or five times before they respond to the booker. I was adamant about reminding models that it is their responsibility to make themselves available from 9AM–on, every day."

The consequences to Louise's advice is that models must focus and realize the importance of having great communication skills with their agents, and being as professional as possible at all times. With the lightning speed of the Internet, competition is fiercer than ever and there are untold numbers of models waiting so snag a job that you might otherwise miss, unless you communicate regularly and are serious about keeping up with technology. End note; be very careful with pursuing modeling on the Internet, there are zillions of scams out there, so try to seek professional advice before you take action.

Another downside of the internet, is that a model of no real substance or qualifications can be successful, simply by the amount of social media presence they have. It has turned into a numbers game, with celebrities overpowering the market. Many models today are not the tall, svelte type that is easily recognizable on the street, but they are somewhat average looking. They are top models simply because they are among the wealthy, have celebrity families, and have hyped themselves up on social media and accrued thousands of followers. These "social media" models probably don't know the difference between silk satin, and crepe de chine as models in my era did, and no idea that it is their job to "sell" the garment. Today, it's about getting people engaged in your "brand" on Instagram, Twitter, Snapchat etc., and how many followers and likes you have, to become a supermodel, and get top bookings. It can be quite deceiving how much these "social media" models are actually working because of the constant publicity. However with this instant gratification and hype, careers are short lived compared to models ten to twenty years ago. With the digital age and social media, it is much easier for models today to get recognition. By my story and other former models' biographies, you see how we had to work much harder to make it. We had to make our own way, totally dependent on our beauty, style and talent.

CHAPTER TWENTY-EIGHT

Get Out and Go for It!

O ne of the many words of wisdom and pieces of advice that I cherished from my mother is about the importance, and the significance of dreams, not only having them, but also interpreting what they might signify realistically. First and foremost, however, she told me to always believe in my dreams, and to dream BIG! From watching the old Bette Davis and Joan Crawford movies or any movie that starred glamorous ladies of the 40's and 50's, (with my Mom's pumps on), which so deeply captivated me from a very early age, was a sign that I was fascinated with fashion and beauty. I would constantly daydream about dressing up, and becoming a movie star one day. Though it didn't happen quite the way I planned, I had a passion for something, recognized my fate, and made it happen!

I knew I had to leave Portland, if I were to ever have any hope of making my dreams come true, and thank God, I had the courage and circumstances to do it; success most times requires change, and leaving your comfort zone. It was not easy, being I was the rebel in the family—no one else in my family, with the exception to some degree of my mother—was even remotely interested in the arts, and I received no early support, guidance, encouragement nor assistance from any of my relatives, aside from my sister Marian a bit later. And though I made some bad decisions—don't we all—I managed to fashion a successful International high-fashion modeling career for myself, despite the tremendous odds of my race, circumstances, inexperience, and the environment in which I found myself. I believe that the single most important component of my success has always been my bold and brazen courage to take a chance, to as they say, "go for it"!

You should be able to recognize from my life history that dreams don't always blossom on the first try, that sometimes it takes two, three, four, or a seeming infinity of tries, before your dreams become reality. I have also learned, as should you, that there are many talented people in the world who never really succeed because they lack one crucial characteristic. Persistence. It is so easy to give up on yourself and your dreams, but use me as your example; I wouldn't recommend taking the daring chances that I did, or leaving your children without a strong family support, due to the dangerous circumstances in the world today. But, believe in yourself, and pursue your chosen career, and don't let anything or anyone stop you, if you really want it.

Modeling has afforded me so many opportunities that I would otherwise never have had, and to see parts of the world that I would have never dreamed that I would have the opportunity to visit. Because of modeling, the acting and music industry also opened itself up to me; Though I never seriously studied it, I learned on the job, and I have appeared in some of the now defunct soap operas, feature films, had the privilege of working closely with some amazing stars of television and the big screen, landed a national TV commercial, and several regional ones as well. As my career was ending in Paris I sang at the iconic Olympia Stadium, opening for then pop star, Sydney Youngblood, and in New York was chosen to sing with the legendary vibraphonist, Lionel Hampton. I followed the signs that let me know I had "it" and as of this writing, I'm enjoying a successful career as a lead singer, doing both cabaret and concerts, while still doing commercial print modeling and coaching!

My coaching technique is very successful, due to the knack I have of drawing out a models best qualities and teaching them how to perfect themselves, the same way that Ruth Turner taught and perfected me. After three decades in the business, I have acquired a keen eye for modeling talent, that hint of latent body language that tells me that someone has "it", which has enabled me to serve as a scout for agents as well. When I spot a potential model, I do everything I can to help direct them into professionalism; there are few joys and satisfactions that can compare to having someone that I have mentored, come to me and tell me what an inspiration I have been, and how grateful they are for the guidance I provided to help jump-start their career.

Not all aspiring models have the coordination or measurements to be a runway model—in point of fact, very few, relatively speaking, do—but after a few sessions under my tutelage, during which I am absolutely candid and frank about their prospects and abilities, at least they will know why they will not succeed in the runway business, and perhaps other aspects of the business would be a better choice. And, without exception, even if my assessment of them is negative in terms of pursuing a modeling career, at least they emerge more self-confident and self-aware, with enhanced self-esteem, and a clear idea of what professional modeling entails. For more information, see my website, shailahedmonds.com

I must mention my disheartenment with the fashion business, for the blatant lack of diversity on the runway. For this reason, and other politics, I never worked for many of the top designers in New York, because they had their quota of black models. Thus the reason I sought refuge in Europe where I was booked for my energy and talent to sell, not on my personal circumstances. Models of racial diversity still have a very hard time establishing themselves in this business. Especially in Europe, where Black models were once the rage, they are now seldom seen. Though there is a hint of change, (thank you designer, Zac Posen, for using a predominately black group of models recently) I only hope it will continue. The discrimination, which still persists, makes me feel as if all my sacrifice, struggles and contributions to the business were for naught; the inroads I made and the doors that I opened for those coming behind me, were all in vain. It is hard for me to enjoy a live fashion show, because the walking styles have become so blandly homogenized, and there are no standout models that I would call superstars. Today, the look is all about not having anything or anyone distract from the garment, being as staid and bland as possible. But, as the saying goes, where there is life, there is hope, and I live with hope and confidence that these setbacks are only temporary, and that the magic that I generated on the runway will return someday, putting the "show" back into the fashion show…soon!

When my hectic schedule slowed down, I had time to have some "me" time. In my quest to connect to my African roots, I married an African drummer, which produced another son, Joseph Kuo II, but the marriage only lasted a few years. Despite being single again, I am happy, and enjoying the wonderful mementos, and beautiful, cherished photographs, that now surround me at home, to remind me of the fabulous life that I was so privileged to live, on the runways of the world. I take humble pride when I realize what it took for me to conquer and prevail in the ultimate modeling venue, the world of the haute couture! It has been my dream to write this book, and it was a great pleasure sharing the details of my modeling life with you. I hope this book has given you a newfound or deeper appreciation, and respect for the modeling world as well as inspiration to succeed. For those of you who are lucky enough to be a successful model, please keep a handwritten journal, so you can look back and cherish wonderful memories, as I had forgotten many great ones, until I reopened mine. When I look at the photograph on the back cover of this book, I revel in the look of sheer exhilaration and joy that it reveals, and in my mind, the caption should read, "Hallelujah, I did it"!

NOW, GO OUT AND FIND YOUR RUNWAY!

Designer: Franklin Rowe   NYC

CPSIA information can be obtained
at www.ICGtesting.com
Printed in the USA
LVHW022332070519
617047LV00008B/185/P